H

Landscaping

The Ultimate Guide To

Design The Perfect Landscape

By

ROBIN DAWSON

Table of contents

Introduction

A landscape comprises of living as well as non-living objects. For example, around your house everything included will be a landscape, usually gardens/plant decorations etc. These are also called the landscape components. Some examples of non-living things can be water, rocks, soil, gravel roads, timber, water beds, flower beds, fire pit, benches, fence, any furniture etc.

As for the living components, the plants and hence the animals inhabiting the area serve as the fine exemplar. The way these components are selected and coordinated together serve as the contrast as to how a landscape may look; good or bad.

Landscaping is divided into two parts; soft landscaping and hard landscaping. Soft landscaping includes all the living features that include plants, trees and shrubs. On the other hand, hard landscaping includes non-living or hard surfaces such as pathways, walkways, entry walk, ponds, streams, statues, sculpture and etc.

Landscapes can be complex and time-demanding to build but with right source of information, techniques and ideas, anyone can master the art of landscaping. Following is the detailed and precise information about how a landscape should be built, what features or materials to use and avoid the themes for landscapes and their benefits and importance.

Chapter 1: Basic home landscaping skills for beginners

A good designer must envision all the possibilities and, alongside being mindful of them, must implement them to improve the impact of one's landscape at home according to how the situation calls them for and the seasons that are in. The following are some basic principles of landscapes that will help you out.

1.1 Seven basic principles of landscaping

The basic principles of landscaping consist of three main components:

1- **Unity:** Unity in landscape compromises of consistency, quality, and repetition of the design. Repetition is used to bring your design together by repeating such elements that contain plants and landscape decoration. Unity is attained through grouping, positioning, or arrangement of several individual components that emanates a sense of similarity hence creating a common theme. An example of this perhaps is, using the same types of plants instead of a range of plants of different color, shape, size, and texture.

The same structural components may also be another exemplar.

Using many different plants or objects may create a chaotic and not very pleasing atmosphere in the landscape.

To create unity is this landscape design, same color continuation; texture, shape, size and proximity of plants are used.

2- **Balance:** In simple terms, balance is a way of achieving equilibrium; equality. The two balances are symmetrical and asymmetrical balance. As the two sides of the landscape are homogenous in symmetrical balance, asymmetrical may agree to differ. In asymmetrical balance, each half is divergent but has similar visual-imaginary weight. Symmetry is of most importance in formal landscape designs.

Symmetrical balance

Asymmetrical balance

In the above pictures, in symmetrical balance identical decorations, plants, and textures, structural components are used to keep the unity in place while in asymmetrical balance a lot of same plants and textures, structural components are used for the sake of unity nevertheless each side differ, making the asymmetry more relaxed while keeping it in order.

3- **Contrast and harmony**: Contrast assists in emphasizing some aspects in the architectural-landscape design, and harmony helps unify aspects of the landscape arrangement. The contrast between the components attracts the attention of the viewer when placed side by side. The collocation of all art elements or the use of vibrant colors is used to accomplish harmony and contrast of the landscape overall.

The contrast in contradiction to harmony must not be exaggerated. Usually, contrasts are used to enhance a feature's attractiveness that passer-by may find pleasing. Some examples are contrasting leaf texture, color or shape and light garden furniture, painted walls, fences that enhance the beauty of the landscape.

Contrast is not only limited to the plants. Other non-living components can also be of use.

4- **Color:** Color gives the element of vibrancy to your landscape pattern and style. Warm, hot colors seem to move towards you, in a way demanding more of your attention (i.e., red, orange, yellow), making the object look nigh. Whilst, cool colors such as green, blue, white, silver, etc. appear to be moving away, giving a more relaxing aura to the landscape; garden

Warm colors

Cool colors

5- **Line:** Lines are of the most important in a landscape, one might like to call them the mother of all. Lines have been made of use to convey a deep and remote illusion also, to highlight an object, influence motion, or focus attention to one specific area or also known as a focal point. The flower bed, edge of a sidewalk, outline of a building, walkways, fire pit, may serve as a fine exemplar.

6. Proportion: The size of one element with respect to the other is proportion. This needs some preparation and thought among all the other landscape principles. All landscape elements must be adequately balanced. The size and scaling of the components must be in proper proportion in terms of the landscape as a whole. For example, large trees or plants may not be proportionate in a small lawn, large furniture in a small space may be awkward from a visual perspective, and a large statue on a small plant may make the plant itself go unnoticed. If done correctly, the proportion can change the overall atmosphere or aura of the landscape to either a dull one or a vibrant one.

7. **Transition:** The transformation in landscape design that indicates the scale and varying plant and color intensity as a gradual change in transition. Color, texture, form, tone, and space are also various forms of transition.

The form is the contour of three-dimensional objects. The extent to which forms are solid is known as mass. The impact of lighter, thicker, or leaves that are darker in color provides the landscape with an enhanced mass. (Plants have varied masses; some might be denser while some are open). When defining space, the volume determined by the boundaries of plants, trees, bushes or shrubs, sky, ground area, and the outer layer of leaves of a group of plants or trees is used (canopy) or hence is space itself. Texture alludes to the components of landscape design: rough or fine, raw, or smooth. The texture is necessary when looking at the size, especially in smaller, more intimate areas. Many different textures are in the wood, gravel, stones, plants, and also water. Tone serves as the connection between the texture, color, and light of the components in a landscape. Different tones change the overall look of a landscape, so one must choose the right tones and colors when designing. Color, as said above, is the correlation between contrast and harmony, the use of cool and warm colors may make a big difference to the landscape.

All of these are also known as design elements.

1.2 Things to avoid and note during landscaping

- Mowing the area will make the landscape look bigger and neat.

- Excess use of contrast and harmony will make the area dull; lack of variety and interest.

- Excess use of contrast will make the landscape look disorderly.

- Bigger spaces will make the area look vacant and hollow.

- Small spaces can make the area appear gloomy and grim.

- A rough texture minimizes the actual size and shape of the area.

- Soft and fine textures enhance the actual size and shape of the area.

- Curved and smooth lines give a sense of passiveness and a friendly aura, they appear pleasant.

- A garden looks vigorous and involved when the lines are uneven, sharp, and straight.

- Bigger trees are to be used to make the garden appear larger

1.3 landscaping effects

1- How to use space:

Splitting the space into series of rooms, areas of a garden can give a more interesting look to a garden instead of a larger area in which you can see every plant, structure, feature, decoration in one glance. Even if your garden is small, you can divide it into two rooms for an overall nourishing and interesting look that one large area will be unable to provide.

Each garden room or area should be typical of one another, so every area/room stands out to a viewer in its own unique and vibrant way, for example using defined structures such as a small pond covered by the outline of flower beds which then leads to a lawn comprised of sitting area, decorated by two statues on either sides or shrubs for a complementary look, etc. The uniqueness of each room, leading to another, will make the viewer curious and compliment the landscape.

Don't overdo with the splitting in order to make a room look distinctive, and a little subtle change will be enough for a room to show its own uniqueness. For example, a lawn lead by the pavement of flower beds to a small traditional planting garden with a little furniture like a table and chair should be enough for a distinctive look or for a more basic as well as the typical look, a little change of level or slightly curved pathways that link one room to another should be a fine exemplar.

2- How to make a garden appear larger

We all have visited a lot of gardens. And some may seem oppressive, with a lack of space and claustrophobic while others appear with a nourishing aura of freedom and large ground to walk on when the mood is dim. Here are some easy techniques that professional designers have used to make a garden look bigger, for beginners that are adamant about home landscaping.

Excess use of sharp and straight lines whilst creating or designing paths and beds will make the area look smaller and boxed. Curved lines serve as an enhancing effect and will make the garden look bigger and quite spacious.

Make use of paths in a way that they gradually narrow when moving away from the main area example where you sit or a veranda. Making use of such a way will create an illusion that the actual distance has increased. Also, textures that are fine and smooth and landscape structures will also further enhance the look and make the garden appear bigger than its original size. For example, the use of pebbles that are in a smaller size on the pavement will give the illusion of enhanced size.

When using mulch on the beds (optional), select smaller sized or smaller particles of it. It also has a low density. It will not overcrowd the bed and will be equally beneficial.

3- How to choose plants

It is an advice to not to put so many plants as it will overcrowd the area. Sometimes less is more, which in return creates an illusion of bigger spaces. Use small and fine-leaved plants in the area that is in the center instead of broad and bigger sized leaves. It is also generally recommended. Wide and broad-leaved plants can be placed in the front of the bed, with foliage that is smaller in size at the back to even the look. Colors can also play quite a big part in how a landscape/garden appears. Warm and hot color flowers, which give off a strong, imposing aura, make the area look smaller, whereas cool colors make the area look bigger as they are not that vibrant and blend easily within the landscape, evening the view and maximizing the comfort level of a viewer.

4- How to use colors

Correct usage of colors and contrast can turn tables on any ordinary-looking garden, making it appear beautiful and memorable. Combining colors can have a greater impact and attract a lot of attention. The greater the contrast, the greater the effect will be. Use colors such as pink and blue, blue or white, yellow, and light green.

Not all of the best contrasts depend on the flowers. Some of it can be by foliage. Make use of foliage like evergreen trees/plants such as Cercis Canadensis, which are pinkish-violet blossoms during spring and heart-shaped leaves of dark purple color when its summer, can make a great impact, and continue to contrast throughout the year. Or using seasonal plants such as deciduous plants for change of looks year-round. Besides plants, the non-living elements can also serve a great deal of contrast; for example, a painted wall, flower pots used for decoration, painted fence, and any garden furniture can create light spots of contrasts.

5- How to use colors to enhance contrasting

Colors that are the same; for example, red is made by mixing orange and pink are not that contrasting and will make the landscape appear dull comparatively if the same colors were to be placed together. Opposite colors are quite contrasting and make an eye-catching view. Some examples of contrasting colors are:

- Dark green with pink and red.

- Yellow with purple or blue

- Light blue with red

- Dark blue with orange

- Yellow with purple and blue

- White with dark green and gold color

- Silver with dark red and purple

Opposite colors have a greater contrasting impact than the colors of the same type.

6- How to apply decorative touches to the area/garden/landscape

Refrain from using large, huge structures for decoration, for example, enormous looking garden furniture, statues and sculptures, huge pots will steal away all the attention from the main area. Make use of light furniture as it will not only give a sense of simplicity; it will also make the area look spacious. Decoration of lightening can give the garden a whole new otherworldly life at night and will create a wonderful view for you to enjoy with a cup of tea.

7- Color and light

Even if a feature is great and beautiful, if lightening is not right, its true beauty can never be appreciated. As they say, light and color are two components that work together to create a greater impact. Vibrant and contrasting colors will change the overall view when penetrated with light sources. For example, flowers that are actually of sapphire blue color during sunset will appear light purple or violet. White flowers, if touched with any artificial light sources, will lit up with a varied color at night. Statues or sculptures during sunlight will appear clear while during the night, if light source present, it will appear like they are shining with an overall effect of the lightening (depends on the color of lightning, how the colors will appear).

Chapter 2: Study Of The Natural Patterns Of The Garden

Anyone who has spent time looking at nature noticed that at many scales, specific patterns — waves, spirals, circles, branches — seem omnipresent and repeat. A branching pattern occurs in the intersection of streams and rivers apparent from a jet plane, in the majestic arch of a tree above and its roots below us, and in the tendrils of a little fungus. Spirals exist in galaxies ranging thousands of light-years, in a daisy's head. We can see ocean movements on colliding storm fronts and on the beach, including in huge swells and fragile ripples. In all these situations, matter and energy are directed to an efficient form to support what needs to happen. Branching patterns are suitable for collecting and spreading resources and materials, and trees are using them to collect heat, distribute water and nutrients. Ripples and waves allow two water bodies to move with limited turbulence. Every time we look at such a pattern, it's the way nature solves a design concept — moving, harvesting, collecting, or dispersing mass and energy in a wonderfully fast and easy way. That's what we're able to achieve with an ecological landscape. And we will research any of these phenomena, see what they may tell us. Humans, too, use patterns, but if voluptuous curves and intricate nature fractals occur in our work, they are there for beauty, not purpose. Ruler-straight circles, checkerboard roads, concrete, and glass grid work, and milled lumber parallelograms are our common patterns. Often such patterns are perfect for the work, but these patterns are uncommon in landscapes. Nature's shapes aren't ever rectilinear, so there's a justification for that. Choosing and installing the correct shapes and design in a landscape, besides producing elegance, will save energy, minimize labor, improve wildlife habitat, and help manage plants, insects, and other species, including gardeners. I'll continue with a basic illustration of how form and design can save us time and energy, and then switch to a couple more complex concepts derived from the patterns of nature.

2.1 Keyhole Garden Beds

A garden's shape defines how much of its field will simply be utilized to produce plants, as compared to pathways to approach certain plants. Any little route is an unusable property that could be committed to a rich polyculture of herbs, vegetables, and sweet-scented flowers. Fortunately, modifying the design used for garden beds will reduce the

land-sacrificed to the path. Changing a garden bed's shape —
working with patterns — can minimize the area lost to paths,
as shown in these beds, each comprising 50 sq. ft. of planting.

Single rows: It requires 40 square feet of path

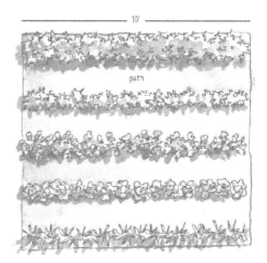

Raised beds: It requires 10 square feet of path

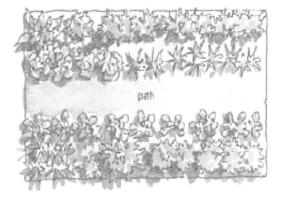

Keyhole bed: It requires just 6 square feet of path

The simple garden bed comprises single rows of plants with pathways between rows. Throughout this layout, paths occupy almost half the soil. A raised bed garden where pathways pass through three or four rows of plants is an improvement, losing just around 30 percent of the land to walkways, thus keeping the beds small enough for the gardener to enter the center. A simple geometry change here has eliminated nearly half of the path space. But while at it, we can do better and build an eye-pleasing template. When we turn the rectangular elevated bed into a circle — or, more precisely, a horseshoe shape — more route will vanish. The route shrinks to a tiny keyhole form by a basic topology trick, giving this space-saving garden arrangement named: keyhole bed. Now here, we cover a standard 4-by-15-foot elevated bed in a U shape along with a small central area for a road, and we cut the path down from about 22 square feet (shaping an 18-inch path down one side of the elevated bed) to 6 square feet. Less than a quarter is surrendered to paths. Keyhole beds have both beauty and mathematics. Introducing curves into a garden reduces the appearance of the "soybean area" from ruler-straight beds and rows. It rarely takes the shortest path between two points, except dropping apples and other gravity-driven phenomena. Instead, nature meanders, drifting from here to there in graceful but effective undulations. Humans have become fascinated by the unswerving, direct route. Yet we meet nature on her own terms in our landscapes. Just as a straight stretch of road encourages narcolepsy, rectangular gardens are also monotonous. Circles and Curves offer a garden delight and whims. What a bonus, too, they happen to be more effective—a keyhole bed with cabbages and tomatoes and side greens and herbs in diameter of 8-10 feet.

A greenhouse mandala. A circular layout of keyhole beds is both lovely and room-conserving.

Further advantages of keyhole beds: if we position the central route to the south and find high plants like sunflowers or tomatoes at the back or north side, the bed produces a U-shaped sun bowl that retains the air. Inside, the toasty microclimate is a nice place for tender or sun-loving variants. Simple to irrigate, too. A simple tiny sprinkler in the middle casts a revolving spray design to drill the pad.

Several keyhole beds can be extended from a center path to make a garden with pleasant curves and reachable bed space.

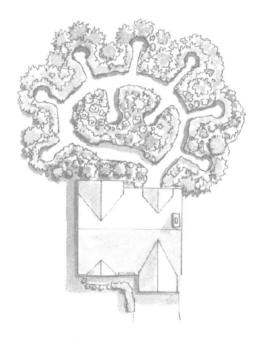

2.2 Other Natural Patterns in the Garden

Below are some more forms in nature that aid gardeners to understand.

A few spiral forms observed in nature.

Branches:

Branching patterns are used to accumulate or distribute resources, electricity, and water. Trees spread leaves across wide areas to better block the sun. Forking roots collect moisture and nutrients. We should add our garden division observation. California artist and trainer Earth flow Design Works' Larry Santoyo frequently utilizes designs in his landscape projects. Driven leaf observation taught him a novel garden path style. Throughout one of his lectures, he transferred leaves to his classmates. "See branching veins," he informs us. "We need the least possible room to bring sap from the green cells to the rest of the farm," he said. The central vein of the leaf was thickest, its major branches half the height, and from those expanded small veinlets for carrying nutrients to and from every cluster of cells. The veins themselves do not catch much energy, so it's best to suppress them. "Why not we plan these garden paths? Why didn't anybody see this? "Asked Larry. "You make a wide main route for a wagon or wheelbarrow, and narrower paths for foot traffic to the tents. You save a lot of room, so you have a perfect flow sequence. "I was struck at how initial Larry's statement was. He designed several popular gardens using this template, and others replicated him.

Branching patterns are an effective way to approach all the points in a broad area, moving as short as possible. Also, a single branch is simple to restore if harmed, so its absence has a limited impact on the entire structure or organism. Wherever selection or dispersal is expected in nature, branching patterns may be found: the tributaries of a river channel, the seed heads of Queen Anne's lace and umbel flowers, the forking zigzag of light bolts, blood vessels, or the ever-finer tubing divisions of a drip irrigation network. Branches are growing in nature and our gardens.

Nets:

Net or net design is used in nature in bird nests, spider webs, honeycombs, and dried mud cracking. Nets are forms of growth, contraction, and distribution. Gardeners also establish a net pattern while putting seeds in a raised bed, positioning seeds in a triangular pattern to build even distances among seeds. This pattern suits most seeds into limited space. Garden routes, shaped after a vine. A leaf's vein design is a room-conserving way to distribute nutrients to the leaf cells without losing precious glare-gathering soil. For a garden's routes, we should follow the same method, reducing the growing area lost to our crushing feet.

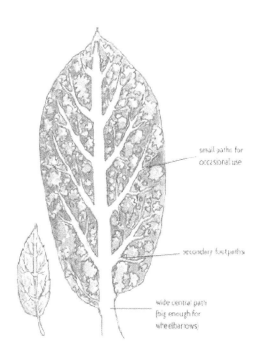

small paths for occasional use

secondary footpaths

wide central path (big enough for wheelbarrows)

A triangular net design enables planting more seeds in the same area than the more widely employed rectangular model.

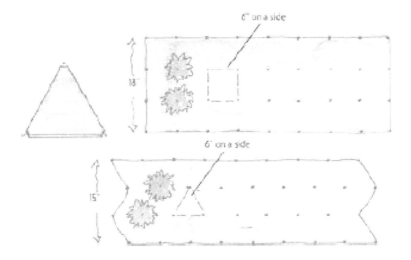

Orchardists grow their trees in a net system in drylands, gathering rain and drainage. Fruit trees are planted in small depressions, and shallow trenches link the basins. Through this innovative device, water flowing over a wide region is gathered by the trench network and distributed to the root of the tree.

Nature uses net designs to create soil, so we may take a leaf from her book for our landscapes. I saw moving sand dunes supported by net vegetation trends. Blustery winds on dunes disperse grass or other seeds uniformly across a wide area; as each plant develops, a tiny shaded, windless patch is formed around it. Supported by this self-created, harmless microclimate, the plant starts sending runners and colonizes a new area. Soon a net pattern of plants captured and restrained a large patch of garden, even though exposed earth lies between the plants. Over time, scattered plants grow and bind together. Then the entire area was "tamed" and moderated, transformed into a gentle, inviting environment. We may use this design on our yards. If our soil is weak and plants are small, the classic solution is usually labor- and money-intensive rush to apply topsoil and cover the site with plants all at once — a technique that typically results in excessive work accompanied by a ton of dead plants.

Chapter 3: The Designing of Landscapes

Let's start with the design approach. When you're finally starting on how to design your landscape, you have to think of an approach. It is necessary to observe the area first and put your plans together because if you don't take the necessary steps to the approach, in the beginning, the whole design will be ruined. The next step is to carefully observe all the elemental components and features in the area and think of how to include them in your final design. For example, if there are rocks included in the landscape, you might be able to use them and create the desired design. Always keep in mind that you're looking for the most efficient way to reach the design you have thought about. And you also do need to ensure that the already present features and structures will suit your new landscape design. And be thoughtful if the area you're designing can afford your desired changes and designs. The most important thing is the 'end look.' For example, every person would want their home landscape to look pleasing to the eye, alongside to solve some practical problems, for instance, poor drainage. So keep everything in mind and go through with a proper and thorough design plan.

Here are some questions you can ask yourself before working on the area:

1- What is the scope of the design?

2- How do you deal with the existing features and structures on the landscape?

3- The design you have considered; does it fit the landscape and its structures?

4- Is there enough space and room for the design you are considering?

5- The design you're considering will make the area look more pleasing?

3.1 Developing of the base plan

- **Purpose:**

Start by creating a good, scaled drawing from a bird's-eye view of your existing landscape. This map should precisely pinpoint the property lines, house, drives,

Fences, utility lines, trees, and other existing components and features that may play a role in affecting the advancement of your landscape. There are quite a number of ways of calculating and recording the elements of your landscape on paper.

Check out one or more of the strategies below.

- **Identification of area/landscape lines:**

This step can be made quite easier if you get the map, which shows you area lines and location of the house on the area or property. Map could be of any kind; a plat, architect's or builder's plan, etc. The map could include the hardscapes and structures that are fixed; houses, exits, entryways walkways, walls, driveways, and so on. Although it mostly depends on where you live, these papers can be obtained with ease with papers that you acquired when you bought your home. If the area lines are difficult to verify, you may have to consult a licensed cartographer to verify the boundaries of the area for your land to test them. The survey plan could also be used as a foundation for the layout that you would be making use of in further steps.

- **Let's get started**

Use a paper for tracing to create a rough drawing of your area/property for the development of your base/plot plan. If your land property is huge, you might want to split the design into multiple sketches or drawings; landscape areas in front, areas in side-view, areas in the backyard, or you could just use a bigger paper. Your scaled drawing should nevertheless show you the typical shape of the area or property. Make sure you mark the road and lines of the property. It is useful to have an arrow to pinpoint the direction of the north.

- **Selecting equipment**

Collect the necessary equipment to accurately record sizes: 50 to 100 ft. Tape scale, erasers, pencils, etc. and a huge clipboard clasping the tracing paper. You can also make use of measuring paper if that is more convenient for you instead of tape scale-measure. You should also have a scale for drawing and a graph paper for converting your rough drawing to a scaled one. It will be convenient if you have another partner to take measurements when using a tape measure. If the help is not available, use a screwdriver to assist you in holding the tape in place when you measure.

- **How to take measurements**

Take the rough drawing of the area and start taking the measurements with the procedure described below.

After taking all the measurements, bring the rough drawing indoors, and a final or an annual base plan should be drawn to the scale. If the property is smaller, a

1-inch scale = 10 feet (engineering scale measurement) or 1/8"= 1 ft. (measured with architect's scale) are correct scales of drawing. Plant beds with a wide range of species can be selected with a 1/4 "architectural scale = 1 meter. This wider scale can be a good way to display better detail. For example, beds near buildings or areas which include hardscape. Floor plans for buildings are often drawn on a scale of ¼" It can also be used for the planting plan as a base map.

An architectural ruler or the measuring scale of an engineer should be used. Art and drafting markets have such supplies available usually.

The base plan should show all the following information:

- All the lines of property

- Water bodies (low areas, ponds, streams, etc.)

- Windows and doors included in the floor plan

- Downpipes, downspouts; drainage system

- Irrigation system (drip line)

- Outlets of electricity outdoors

- Units of air conditioning

- Outlets of water outdoors

- Meters and connections and boxes of utility

- Decks

- Overhangs

- All fences and walls, any poles, etc.

- Swimming pools (if any), roads, paths, courtyards, forecourts, yards, verandas, any area for parking, entryways, etc.

- Any utility, above and underground, also including

- Telephone, water, electric, septic, gas, sewer, field drains, any tanks.

- Already present vegetation and most importantly large trees

- Size of the scale of the base plan

- All directions (north, west, south, east) shown by a compass.

3.2 Final base plan

(Assuming you have already taken all the necessary measurements, identified all the property lines, located house on the property, located landscape features, measured curved areas and angled features)

Use the graph paper to draw the final plan making use of the biggest scale that fits your area of property. For instance, 100 foot by 70 foot will adjust correctly on a 10 x 10 sq. inch graph paper x 8 1/2 x 11 piece, When 1 "= 10 feet scale is used. Graph paper is available at book shops and sections of office that supply the stores. Create the final plan (base plan) by drawing a line along the centre of grid to show the edge of your road and streets in front of the house. Another line should be drawn to portray the street on the side if you have a lot corner. Then mark the direction of your compass on the final plan with an arrow indicating the north. Put east, west, and south in the relevant area.

All restrictions, facilities, and right of ways should be found that are connected with your area or property. Most cities have sidewalks located on the city area or property, and the property line of the homeowner sometimes begins in the sidewalk or near it. Avoid planting on areas mostly used for street expansion such as easement area.

Pinpoint the line of the front of the property after distance to the easement is determined and gently draw on the paper you're using. Sketch the side and boundaries at the back after that. In case the boundaries at the side do not seem to be parallel, then the boundary line at the front should be drawn. After that, by the usage of the sightline, the back-boundary line can be drawn. By doing this, side boundary or boundary at the side can then be pinpointed. These four boundary lines are necessary to draw for a correct outline of the property, so be careful.

You can now sketch in your house by pinpointing the corner you previously measured for your rough drawing. It will have a certain distance from the closest property line and from the street/road. Find the corner from the graph paper by counting the squares. Then draw your home's measurements and shape. Make sure you pointed out the widths and heights of the window, doors, and the height of windowsill from ground level.

For the next step, shift all the features, including those that will have an impact on the design of your landscape in your rough drawing or sketch.

For drawing the feature that is curved, onto the final plan. Shift all the dot measurements with the area, including a curved edge from the tracing paper to scaled drawing.

Approximate the curved line by using a French curve. You can get a French curve from office supply shops. By rotating the French curve, have at least three points touched, which you have pinpointed by the outer and inner edge of the curve. Accurate representation of your feature is done by this curve line.

After you're done adding all the components and features, your property's base plan will be quite precise and correct. But if you fail to add all the features in one base plan, you always can create another one, which is like an inventory sheet.

If the base plan is created on the tracing paper, it could be quite convenient as you can place it over the base plan for a finalized drawing of your property.

This finished base plan will serve as your go-to map when you're finally creating your landscape.

All the following things should be included in your base plan:

- The precise and correct boundary line of property

- Accurate whereabouts of house, walkways, driveways, fences, courtyards, verandas, yards, porches, and so on.

- Variety, kind, whereabouts of all plants and trees

- Outdoor outlets, electric outlets, and poles, meters

- Cleanout excess ports or location, lateral line of sewer, water and gas

- Cables of TV and cables on the telephone. All of the above or underground

- Utility hole in sewer and fireplug

- All directions north, east, south, and west by a compass

- Types of soil and all of their characteristics

- Architectural designs of the already present neighbourhood or buildings

- Location of the drainage system

- Downspouts, door, and windows, etc.

3.3 Site analysis

Site analysis is an important and necessary step to take. For example, analyzing the conditions of plants, soil, and the overall area is important for further modifications and improvements you want to make to the landscape to enhance the beauty and make the utmost use of the beauty of nature.

Take a new sheet or piece of tracing paper and put it over the base plan. Trace 'all' the features and components of the base plan. This second copy will serve as your site analysis map and will help you further your advancements on the site.

Now let's get started.

- **How to record a landscape?**

The next paragraphs will help you monitor sun characteristics and patterns accurately, shade, water, noise, soils, the shape of the property, drainage of surfaces, and scenery. Mark all the estimated whereabouts of every item and thing and their conditions. Make use of arrows to specify the views, slopes, etc. Have a look at what you have built up till now. It should probably look like your property now.

See the spaces and the correlation between them. Is the area where you usually park too close to the door you mostly use? You might notice that some areas are incompatible with being used simultaneously. Is the view from your living room's window, the piles of wood and tools your neighbor has been hoarding from quite a while? Let's hope that's not the case. To avoid such views and inconvenience, you must mark and specify all the areas that are included in your landscape. A precise and detailed site analysis will do wonders when you progress to further design steps.

- **Understanding the features of the environment**

Movement of sun throughout the days and seasons is an important thing to note for the development of shaded and open areas. Also, do not forget the movements of the sun during winters. Specify with arrows how the winter sun affects your home so that you could have suitable shaded areas for summers and open areas for winters where sunlight can reach and keep the area warm during winters.

- Winds are another important factor to consider. As they can be harsh when the weather is not so good. Note the overall orientation of the wind and place screens in places where the direction of prevailing winds is to protect you from bad weather.

- State the areas that are most impacted with the surrounding noises on your analysis sheet/plan. Noises from neighborhood, nearby subways, can really impact your quality time for relaxing. One way to avoid noise is to place shrubs and trees. They help in minimizing the noises to an extent.

- Another main factor to consider is the kind of soil you're using as your foundation. It can significantly affect the conditions of your foliage and grass lawns. Look at the soil around your house. A soil or a ground test should be carried out every 20 feet on the sides. Avoid collecting mortar or cement chips as it could destroy your plants. Remember to remove these substances before you prepare the soil. If you do not know how to take a sample and submit it, try to contact the extension office for help. They will provide you with a sheet full of instructions and also sample boxes of soil, which can be of great help.

- Surface drainage should be included in your analysis sheet. Make a note of how and where your water flows out of your property and into the property. Or are there other areas where water is flooding into your property. Take a note of the area where water is continuously standing for quite an extended period. And importantly, do add the areas where eroding is happening. The best way to mark your observations is during multiple rainfall occasions.

- The visibility of views seen from all the directions from within your house and from your property should be determined by the site analysis. Specify these on the notes of your analysis.

Take a look at the checklist before you proceed to the next step:

- Movement and patterns of the sun during all the seasons

- Sites of water drainage system; spigots, pipes, areas where water usually drains, downspouts, etc.

- Areas where the surface is low, water usually stays, erodes, the surface is usually soggy

- Areas where water stays

- Screens to avoid noises

- Areas where the wind usually blows

- Areas of erosion

- Areas needing shades

- Warm areas, cold areas, areas where shade is already present

- All the areas within the property where slopes are present; hills, knolls, etc. Everything should be mentioned.

- All the views from the property; good or bad.

- States of all the trees plants and shrubs etc.

- Things that need to be fixed example patios, fences, etc.

- Remove any toxic, harmful plants

- Highly valued fauna and habitat reserves

- Features that need to be fixed or improved

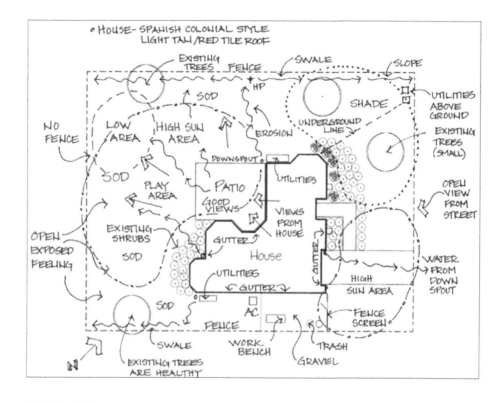

3.4 Wants and needs of your family

With a thorough and comprehensive plan of the site, you're prepared to list your expected areas for use now. The needs of every family member may differ, for example, activities done outdoors.

Followings are the type of places that you might want to consider adding in your landscape:

- Areas for your pet's example stalls or a big lawn

- Entertainment zones

- The area where you could sit and have a nice sunbath, read books

- A swimming pool for water activities

- A little storage room for tools or any kind of equipment

- Sidewalks, gardens, paths

- Any kind of water feature

- Areas you might want to do some cooking, for example, an outdoor barbeque party

- A small lounge for a sitting area

3.5 Areas for outdoor uses

Your property's outdoor areas should tie in with the areas and the activities inside your house. Outdoor cooking zones, for example, would be near the indoor kitchen or the dining room. Areas of service and storage should be located away

from primary areas of use, and from home views. Decks, verandas, patios are to be connected directly to the main entrances of the house.

On another tracing paper, sketch the places where all of these use areas could suit and their estimated sizes. Use many different forms or schemes until you have the best design or layout.

The following figure is an example:

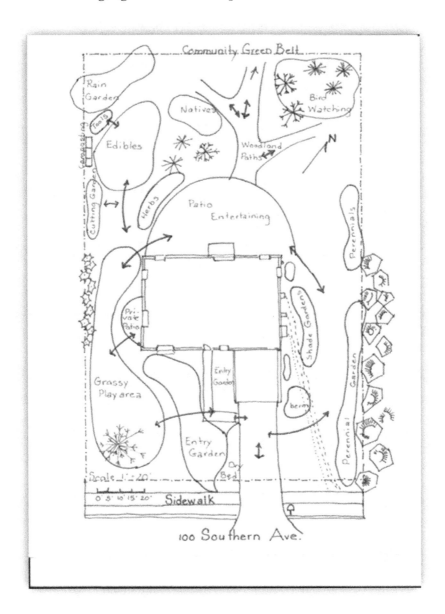

3.6 Developing the outdoor use areas

Each one of the areas for outdoor usage is easier to build if developed individually and afterward combined into the final plan. For example, for designing the space for patios, first of all, decide which elements would make a good area for seating purposes. You can include chairs, tables, and a small roof for a shade, overhangs, garden fountains, or anything else you might like. Review your idea file for the design of the home landscape, any magazines, articles, or visiting areas with a good set up of landscape may provide you with wonderful ideas to develop your own. Keep in mind the instructions and techniques from site analysis, so when you're developing the areas, they do not incline with other elements such as drainage system for water, sewer, pipes, lines for utility, etc. After choosing the size of the space that you think is the most suitable, shift this outline to the plan you're using for landscape with an accurate scale.

Every room of the house has a ceiling, a wall, and floors. In the same way, every landscape area should include all of these things, too, just like how a house has rooms for sleeping, bathing, sitting, for every individual activity. Every landscape also consists of spaces for its respective purposes—for example, places for relaxation, gardening, playing, etc.

Ceilings for outdoor usage are mostly overhangs. It could also be a huge canopy tree's branches that are overhanging the space. Bricks or pebbles may be used as floorings to make the texture of the ground rich. You can find a lot of paving materials that may provide a wealth of patterns and colors for the landscape. Ground coverings are suitable for areas that are seldom trodden and can contrast strongly with products of hardscape that are in a close range. Fences or sides of the building can give privacy. The "walls" may be built of stone, cement, concrete, wood, brick, and also metal. Walls that are 6 ft. can hide the views from adjacent sides. A horizontal slat fence made of wood may provide you with privacy and, at the same time, will invite light breezes to freshen your mood. Evergreen plants may be thick enough to provide you with privacy, and yet they will let the airflow to your area. As every room of a house has courts, yards, halls, and doors, so does the area of landscapes like paths and entryways. Placing gates is an easy and useful way for the separation of outdoor areas.

An inviting and beautiful entrance to a courtyard can be created by the use of pergolas. This way, a patio can also be separated from the entrance and lawn.

Garden rooms are made for relaxing, sitting, and having fun. That is if the garden rooms are comfortable enough. For instance, in the southern areas, the atmosphere is very hot, so it is a necessity to have shade. If you have also created or considered creating a social place, then have seats or sofas, tables for serving food, and maybe some lighting for functions during the night. Consider arranging seating area for social or even private gatherings in corners or a narrow space for more privacy and for the sake of avoiding traffic paths. The best way for the creation of personal spaces is to keep all the things limited to the size of the people who will usually use them. For example, an ornament for the wall in a huge garden will get unnoticed. So the best way to avoid that is to use a small area for arts and ornaments that are detailed.

Water features are the best decorations out there to decorate your gardens with. It could be still or flowing; for example, a small fountain with flowing water, a still pond with little lilies. It gives a whole new life to your garden. Sculptures or any other elements that you like can be added in small places of the garden or even courtyards. You can also add fireplaces to the area you have reserved for cooking for the night gatherings. Spaces that are small also play a part in magnifying the texture of plants.

Plants and bamboos are plants that are rich in texture as they grow very tall, so they do not take a lot of room and grow out of bed area that is narrow. And so they create the best place for planting flowers that are rich in fragrance such as jasmine, roses, tuberose, and viburnum. Fragrances are somewhat absorbed into the walls too, so you can enjoy the light and beautiful rich scents. Rich and light scents are also said to improve one's mood and to create a relaxing environment. A few use areas that you can consider:

1- Parking areas and driveways

Your driveway may already be present, but if provided with practical solutions, they can still be changed. It all depends on how you want your guests and yourself to be welcomed into your home. Do you want to have flower beds in front of the entrance to the driveway, do you want to add more edges to the pavements when you're getting out of the car, do you want to have large trees or small plants to welcome you to your house? Do you want the driveway and parking areas to be separated from the entryways that walk you home? All of these suggestions depend on your personal preferences, which will add to your quality of life.

2- Drives and walkways

Add walks where you think they are a necessity. Include them along the streets, or you could add them to the street, so it connects to your home. Before you consider adding any type of paving material that is permanent, check your location and the setback lines. There are many varieties of materials used for paving for drives and walks. The important thing that you have to consider is what type of paving material you want to use. They are of two kinds; permeable and impermeable. Pavements that are permeable are designed to filter storm water, rainwater, or any water that might have built up, into the soil or through drain tiles. They generally include porous asphalt, pervious concrete, and interlocking pavers, unmortar brick on the sand, and paving stones. They are also mostly used in driveways, walkways, sidewalks, and so on. Impermeable obviously means that the water cannot filter or pass through. Developed areas with substantial quantities of impermeable pavements experience serious water quality issues and are having problems with water falling aquifers. Due to these water problems, there have been limitations on the installation of impermeable paving in the construction of sites.

You should attach the front walk to your front entrance to where the parking area is or simply to the street. You can also think about providing a path from the public outdoor space to the private area, so visitors don't have to step in your house to reach the backyard area for parties. The form of pathway or walkway should be the same as the one used for the main type in the general design. For instance, if you used curved planting or flowering beds, consider using curved walkways too for a categorized look. Wide walkways are more comfortable than narrow ones. If we were to calculate the minimum, a 4 and 1/2 ft. is quite wide for two people to walk together. For adding an interesting look to the walkways, you can add steps, ramps, or retaining walls. Despite providing an interesting look, it will also be comfortable for people who have difficulty walking or are disabled, etc. Consult a professional to help you with this.

3- Main entrance

Let's talk about the main entrance of the house. If the front lots are comparatively smaller, then the most attention gaining component is the gate. The balance of the front composition is determined by the quality and richness of the front entrance. In other words, all the other elements should enhance the beauty of the front entrance rather than competing for attention. Analyze the appearance of your house. See if both sides are visually balanced. For example, one side may look heavier whilst others appear to be light. Light as in one side has larger and heavier plants while the other side is plain. The key to a front entrance that is rich in quality aspects is the way the front entrance is visually balanced.

4- Combining everything together

The form used for areas outdoors should appreciate and enhance the features, structures, and architecture of the house. It is recommended that all the structural elements, architectural structures, both outdoors and indoors, should follow a common design/form. For instance, if the shape of the house is rectangular, then all the patios, verandas, walls, fences, water features, flowers, or planting beds should be of the rectangular form too. Using a common form and design invests in the simplicity and harmony of the design. Moreover, different forms might be complex and difficult to achieve successfully. Make a preliminary plan on another sheet of tracing paper, and visualize and draw your ideal version of space (to correct scale). Keep visualizing and making improvements to your space until you have finalized the look that meets your desired design.

3.7 Planting plant symbols

Thinking about which plants you want to use in your landscape design may seem overtiring in the beginning and might take a toll on your brains, especially if you are a beginner in home landscaping. Make use of your site analysis layout that you developed during previous steps and select the plants that suit the conditions of your landscape's microclimates, which are sunny, moist, dry, well-drained, etc. It would be convenient to make a list of the microclimates found in your landscape for the correct selection of the plants. For instance, if the beds in front are getting full sunlight, then choose plants that require the most sunlight for the front beds after you're done making the microclimate list, select plants that incline with the microclimates, and then choose the ones that interest you.

Following is the information required for you to find the plants:

- Requirements of light

- Growth rate

- Size of maturation/when matured

- Requirements for maintenance

- pH level and moisture of the soil

- Tolerance to heat

- The degree to which they are susceptible to pests and other diseases

- Hardiness zone of plants

- Planting palettes

Once you have found and selected the plants suitable to use, make a list in which you place them into categories they fall in. For instance, tall, medium and small shrubs, tall trees, groundcovers, creepers, accent plants, canopy trees, and specimen.

This will serve as your 'plant palette' in your planting plan when you're selecting plants. It will be convenient to also insert photos of each plant as well as a symbol that portrays its moisture, dryness, amount of light, and other preferences they might have. When you're done with categorizing plants into a group, you will be able to the suitable microclimates for them. This is a reliable way to find many combinations of plants and to find which combinations of plants work best with the texture and color of each other.

- Uses of plants

Plants have many uses too. So be mindful and have full knowledge of the plants you're selecting. For example, if you have to cover up a view, you might want to select tall trees and shrubs that are evergreen. Think about the functions you want plants to serve you. Plants are also capable of providing you with more than one use. For example, the shrubs and trees you have planted to cover the view may also serve you with different kinds of fruits such as pears, raspberries, and blueberries. And they may also be the perfect shelter and habitat for wildlife. Other than that, plants can provide you with varieties of strong, light, or medium fragrances and also cut flowers.

- Themes

Everyone is looking for beautiful themes for their landscapes. There are many landscape themes that you can choose from. They mostly include the types of flower beds you want to plant. Beds used for landscape are made up of a collection of plants that follow one common theme. Some examples are English cottage-style garden, English country style garden, Japanese Zen style, and many more. (All of these are described in chapter 'Themes for landscapes'). If you enjoy flower arranging and want to create cutting beds, you might want to plant perennials and annuals as they are mostly only grown for their beautiful blooms if you want to attract wildlife to your yards such as butterflies, birds and other wildlife. You may wish to create a wildlife habitat backyard. These gardens are more suited for private areas than the public ones. They are mostly located in the backyard with a little sitting area too.

Things you need to consider before planting:

- Avoid overcrowding your landscape/garden with too many plants. Plants that are placed closely may look eye-catching, but they are at a greater risk for catching diseases and pests because of poor circulation of air. You would like to have a landscape that has a long lifespan rather than replacing the plants after every few years. Remember the maturation sizes of the plants before you start with your planting, which is to be used in the foundation of your plantings, also known as a foundation planting. The beds placed at the entrance and the ones that surround your property serves as the first impression to the guests as they are visually critical. Consider planting trees that have broad crowns away from the buildings, so they have enough room for growth. Estimate a tree's mature width that you have selected to grow and divide it by 2. Go and measure the distance you have calculated from the building and mark it. You will have the minimum distance for the tree's center on your plan. If you're using accent plants, then it's preferable to put them on the corners and also in front of the walls that are blank. If you overcrowd the planting near your entrance, then they will definitely grow out of proportion and will exhaust you with an extensive amount of maintenance. Use color and texture in front of the entrance or the front door for an eye-catching loo. However, you don't have to use a lot of varieties or a range of colors for an eye-catching look. A small number of colors can have a huge impact too. You can plant shrubs according to their sizes, from highest to lowest and vice versa. Groundcovers or shrubs with small heights look good when planted along the edges of the bed.

- Keep a distance between plants and the house siding area, drip lines, and eaves because if it's overcrowded with plants, siding can rot. Most importantly, never spread mulches that are organic over termite treatment band neither should you dig into them. Beneath house eaves, dry soil is a problem if no gutter is present. The force from which waterfalls can significantly damage plants, also causes the soil to splash against the base of the house, also eroding the soil. The use of limestone and river rock gravel that is placed below the drip line helps with the drainage problem and also minimizes the water damage.

- Evergreen hedges that are dense wouldn't be a recommendable choice to be used for screening air conditioning units as they not only demand frequent pruning, they also reduce access and the flow of air to the units. Using informal plants with an open structure that is placed away from the units would be a wise choice instead. Be careful when you're selecting screening units. If your screening units are only visible from one angle, then the usage of a one-sided unit is recommended. Some units also have one, two, or three sides, for instance, lattice screens, and they are also very effective. You can also consider the usage of vines if you have selected lattice screens, it's optional.

- Sunshade and exposure can be challenging if you wish to place landscape beds on both sides. Some houses have a contrast of sunshade and exposure along the entrance of the residence. For example, full sun conditions exist on one side while a huge tree may be providing shade to the specific area on the other. Chameleon species that survive in both sun and shade conditions can be placed to achieve a visual, formal balance and for an overall balanced and unified look.

- Plants can be formal or informal. Asymmetrical beds or curvilinear beds are classified as informal, while symmetrical beds or which have angles are said to be formal. Moreover, plants that are even in numbers typically have a formal appearance, while plants that are odd in numbers appear to be informal. Plants having same numbers are also either formal or informal; it mostly depends on their arrangement. You can find templates in the drafting section of the office supplying store. Look at the scale to which your base map has been drawn to. If it's drawn on a scale of 1 inch = 10 ft. (using an architectural scale) and the size of the maturation of your plant is 5 ft., then you should select a circle that measures half an inch (1/5 or .5). Likewise, when measuring groundcover, that measures 2ft. you will select a circle measuring 1/5 of an inch (1/2 or .2). For a small accent tree, the measurement may be up to 10-15 ft. or could be more depending on the species. So you will choose the symbol width accordingly to its maturation size. Be careful when drawing the symbol widths as the thickness of the pencil's lead can affect the width size. Planting symbols are usually just simple circles, but to represent different characteristics of the plant, you can modify the circles for differentiating. For example, you can modify the circles to show a branched appearance for the deciduous plant. You can sketch evergreen plants with needles and sharp edges, while evergreen plants that are broadleaved can be shown with rounded edges. In the same way, for accent plants, you can draw a plant symbol according to its typical texture. Focus on how you can depict the characteristics of each plant with a specific symbol that you can recognize when you're referring to your plan.

- You should be very careful about spacing plants. Knowing and considering a plant's mature size is of utmost importance. For instance, it wouldn't be recommendable to place a plant 3 ft. apart knowing that it's mature size will be 5 ft. When placing several grouping of plants that are of different species together in one bed, refrain from placing the masses of plants too close to each other so they can have ample room to grow and transition. Sketch your planting symbol that represents each plant's mature size and avoid placing them too close. Also, do not forget to leave enough space for access and maintenance of utilities like utility meters and so.

- Deciding on which plant to locate as the first one on your plan may seem exhausting at first. You might find yourself in the shoes of a painter with a blank mind and an empty canvas. However, it's not that difficult if you follow the steps logically and start locating elements that are more important than the others on your landscape. Start with the plants that are strong and have the most impact; trees, focal points, or accent plants. Followed by the plants that will play the supporting cast of enhancing the important plants in aspects of beauty and attractiveness.

- Let's focus on focal points. Focal points are the points that command the most attention from the eye. They can be any non-living structural components or living components such as plants. Specimen trees, statues, sculptures, ponds may serve as some of the exemplars. A focal point can be an individual plant that is dominant than the others or a surprising structural feature that immediately commands the attention of the eye. Focal points are mostly located to provide the landscape (all the elements that surround it) with an overall visual balance.

Take into account the functions of the plants that you're locating on your landscape. Your brand-new empty lot with no trees may demand the planting of canopy trees for shade. Or the use of evergreens for covering an undesired view, throughout the seasons. Consider which kind of trees you are planting in your residence. Especially when you're planting large trees, for example, evergreens can physically overcrowd and dominate your residence if placed too close to the structures. Avoid planting large trees that might grow too big for your residence and also make it hard to access the utilities. Make use of trees that will not only appear small but will also stay in proportion to your house's scale. If you're planting large trees, you have to take into account their root zone and leave enough space for them to grow. Also, if you're planting under trees that are already present, use utmost care as you can disturb the roots of the tree, which may cause root loss, and in a worst-case scenario, you might even cause the tree to die if you were not careful.

- Did you know that accent trees serve as secondary focal points? They usually have strong colors, textures, and forms that catch the eye immediately. The focal point, for example, a specimen tree, maybe a dominant structure in a landscape, but accent plants can be repeatedly planted and provide the landscape with a healthy harmony and contrast as well as unity.

- When you have placed all the dominant structures, focal points, accent plants, and other elements. Start filling the nearby places that are empty. Repeated combinations of shrubs and small plants will not only unify the landscape but will also invest in harmony.

- If there is space left on your planting plan, it would be convenient to include the common name or the Latin name, its size, height, and quantity. This will reduce the time taken for finding the plant symbol on the plan as well. But sometimes the plan does not always have enough space for all the information. However, there's always a shortcut technique available. You can use the first letter or two of the plant's name and the quantity. For example, if the plant is Coral Cactus, you can write it as 'C-12' or 'Co-12'.

- It is recommended to create a plant key in which you will include all of the plant symbols, their Latin and common names, and sizes of the plants that you're planning to buy on your landscape. You should also include the quantity of every plant you have used in your landscape plan. You might choose to write their short names (the shortcut technique described above). The whole naming system should be clear to you, or else you might get confused when you're finally going along with installation.

Are all of these things included in your landscape plan?

- Trees that provide you with shade during summer and sun exposure during winters?

- Large trees (example evergreens) that are responsible for protecting you from strong winds, particularly from winter winds? (Make sure you plant these in the west and north sides of your property).

- Do you have shrubs and evergreens that are dense for covering unenviable views?

- Do you have accent trees that draw people's eye towards your residence?

- Are the plants placed accurately, considering their mature size to prevent any overcrowding?

- Have you selected the right quantity of plants?

- Are there seasonal plants that will provide you with foliage, color, contrast, and blooms during their respective seasons?

- Does your plan have the correct placement of trees for the clear view of your residence's entrance?

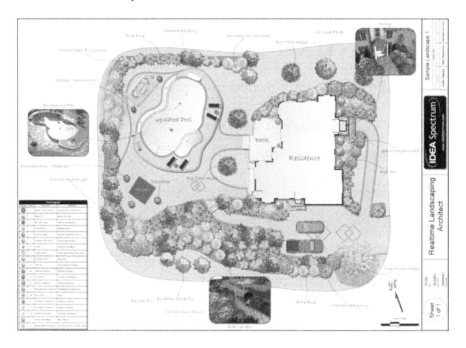

A complete landscape plan is taken from the idea spectrum site.

3.8 Create priorities before you implement

It is recommendable to make a list of priorities you want to include in your landscape after you're done with developing plans for use areas and planting areas. Decide which specific areas you want to develop first considering the time and budget you have on your hands. Consider the following points before plan implementation:

- Plant trees first as they take time to mature

- Land leveling should be finished before any kind of installation is done.

- Grade changes

- It is a wise idea to repair any drainage or water problems before any installation is done.

- Finish all the hard structures and surface elements that are permanent first. For example, pathways, walkways, patios, etc.

- How to create a low maintenance landscape?

  Many people exhaust themselves due to excessive maintenance of the landscapes, and so many seek ways to reduce the workload required for maintenance. The best solution to encounter such a problem is to create a low maintenance landscape that doesn't demand much of your attention and hence is easily managed. For a low maintenance landscape, it is necessary to have a precise, detailed plan created with proper planning, choices that are wise, and the plan that overlooks all the existing and future problems. Specifying the areas that are easily managed and are more manicured is one way of reducing the workload required for the maintenance. Below are some techniques, design strategies, types, and choices of the plants, soil, etc. to help you minimize the excessive maintenance required for the landscapes.

Minimize the unused lawn area

Everyone wants to have beautiful lawns, but unfortunately, they are not only expensive but also requires an immense amount of workload for maintaining their beauty; that is watering, mowing, de-thatching, fertilizing, use of herbicides, pesticides, and fungicides, aerating, liming, lawn edging and raking. Particularly, lawn edging and raking require a huge amount of workload needed for the maintenance to keep the lawn healthy and fresh, which can take a toll on you physically. However, there are ways to achieve a beautiful lawn without too much work. Homeowners stress upon having a proper play and open areas for their lawns, but if lawn area that is unused is removed, then it can save a significant amount of time that is needed for maintenance. Shrubs, trees that are easy to care for, and groundcovers serve as the best alternatives for a lawn that is open and big as they do not require too much care. You can also apply herbicides to the unused area of the lawn, planting wood plant species that require a low amount of care, and planting a layer of mulch of groundcovers can also save time and hard work. Use good quality and long-lasting materials for landscape.

When you're choosing, repairing, or replacing any structural features for the landscape, select materials that are of good quality, last longer, and will not require changing after every few years. Driveways, walkways, patios, entryways, gazebos, fences, sidewalks, decks, any seating furniture, or other furniture you are planning to use should be of good quality, so they are durable. Patios that are made of bricks or concrete mostly lasts for 20-30 years as compared to brick on the sand patio, and a deck made of wood may expire in after approximately 6-8 years. Plastic lumber that has been recycled has much longer durability. Railroad ties or timbers used for landscape have less durability as compared to bed edgings that are created by using concrete and bricks. Blocks of stone edgings also have a longer lifespan. Moreover, mowing strips are used for bed edges that are near to turf areas to limit bed edging treatments. Most importantly, calculate and consider the costs for all the landscape materials, their maintenance costs, costs in the long term future, and the lifespan of all the things you wish to use.

Perennials or annuals?

Choose perennials over annuals for greater color and contrast.

Also, annuals need frequent replacements as they only last one season and so are costly as well where perennials last 'through the years.' Replanting or replacement every year of your begonias, marigolds, petunias, and impatiens mostly depends on the plant's hardiness zones. Choose Walker's low, Geranium Rozanne, Daylilies, Pruning tip, Evening Primrose, Coreopsis' Full Moon', Coneflower, Black-eyed Susan, Astilbe, Stroke Aster for long-lasting colors.

Refrain from choosing high maintenance plants

High maintenance plants require daily applying of pesticides, herbicides, and water to grow well and healthy. Boston Fern, Hybrid Tea Roses, Azalea, Wandering Jew are exemplars of high maintenance plants. Choose plants that can survive in extreme hot and cold temperatures, dry and wet periods, poor soils, does not require regular applications of pesticides and herbicides, are resistant to diseases and insects.

Usage of geotextiles to control weed

Common names for geotextiles are weeding fabrics and land fabrics. They are usually used to minimize the growth of weed in planting beds. For the reduction of weed species, place the fabric on the ground where shrubs are already present and cover it with a heavy layer of mulch. Before covering the

weeds that already exist, herbicides are used. Weed fabrics are permeable and so allow the water and fertilizers to flow through the cloth. They also let air through so plant roots are not short of oxygen. Avoid using a plastic sheet for covering as it not permeable.

Place plants according to their sizes

Placing plants according to their sizes is very important to avoid any inconvenience and extra workload. If a plant surpasses the desired height the area initially required, it might block the view and can also demand frequent pruning, which can be tiring. It is important to know the sizes of the plants when they mature so you can avoid such problems. Ask the owner of the nursery to refer you plants that will not exceed the desired height or width of the area that is required. Locate the fast-growing plant in the rear of the beds or sites of perimeters so they can grow to their mature size and will require minimum to no pruning.

Do not place plants individually

Combinations of plants not only give harmony, contrast, and unity but are also effective if they are placed in masses. You can place mower along the outside edges of a large bed with borders of dense shrubs. It also reduces the usage of weeding and edging.

Keeping the landscape simple

We all know that simplicity is the way to go. Don't overdo with the decoration as a complex design with a variety of different plants; structural elements will naturally ask for much-specialized care. It can be expensive and may require an extensive amount of maintenance. You should always aim for unity and balance. The landscape should beautify your home and not dominate it. A simple landscape can create a carefree and light atmosphere.

- More information on landscaping materials

Landscapes are of two types; hard landscape and soft landscape. The hard landscape consists of structural components, for example, ponds, statues, fences, walls, water features, etc. Soft landscaping consists primarily of plants, trees, and shrubs.

- **Soft landscaping materials:**

- **Plants**

A frequent landscaping mistake is to distribute a variety of incompatible plants in unsuitable growing conditions. They will, therefore, fail to develop to their full potential, and the outcome may result in them dying. Placing a plant that

survives in the sun, in a shady area will result in a weak, scrawny plant and eventually that plant's death.

Consider picking those plants for the front yard that could showcase interest throughout the year. This is achieved by choosing plants that are of interest for many seasons. An ideal deciduous of the non-evergreen plant will have beautiful leaves, flowers of summer or spring, strong color in the fall, and a fascinating shape or branch habit. Look for plants whose interests are not limited to just one season. Evergreen plants might be a nice choice to include, as in the winter months when the deciduous trees shed their leaves, they help to give stability and color. But try to achieve a good balance, as the dominance of evergreens can make the landscape look too dull.

A lot of books and also many software programs characterize plants by design features, effective uses, and cultural needs. Plants that are local to the specific region are the finest option because they have adapted themselves naturally to the local environment and look inherent.

- **Trees**

Trees can be used for many purposes; for example, trees provide us with shade; they clear the air by absorbing odors

and pollutant gases such as sulfur dioxide, ammonia, nitrogen oxides, ozone, etc. and their leaves and bark help in filtering particulates out of the air. Trees also help in cooling the environment around them. They increase atmospheric moisture. They prevent water pollution by reducing runoff, which also helps in preventing soil erosion. They provide food and shield us from UV-B by reducing their exposure by 50%. They also provide habitat for wildlife. They can also be used to enclose the landscape, for covering undesired views and adding interests to shrub beds. So be careful where and how you plant trees.

For a unified or balanced outlook of your landscape, choose trees that are suitable for the overall appearance of the landscape. Choose the place or location based on their mature size. Large trees should be placed in the front of the yard, but as they can dwarf houses, it is important to place them at a distance from the building. People often plant a young tree in very close proximity to the house, and because of that, the tree is not able to grow to its full potential and size.

- **Shrubs**

Shrubs alongside trees form the base of the plantations at the front side of the yard. Look for a blend of deciduous, evergreen broadleaf and shrubs that are of a coniferous kind to give interest throughout the year but refrain from using a large number of different kinds. How or where shrubs are placed immensely affects their looks. To maximize their effect, group the shrubs together in the form of beds or borders. Placing shrubs in groups and masses invests in harmony and increases the overall flow. When plants blend with each other, eye moves across the landscape rather comfortably. When planting, do not forget the shrub's maturation size. If plants are not overcrowded, they can build a nice mass. Locate shrubs so they can start to unite together as soon as they are nearly 70 percent of their overall mature size.

If you're unsure of mature size, refer the books on or any nursery. Shrubs should be planted in the form of odd numbers, for example, five and seven, to increase the quality and composition of the massing. But if you are attempting to establish asymmetrical and formal patterns, even numbers aim to reduce the unity of the placement of plants by visually subdividing the eye. The addition of a fifth or seventh plant results in the grouping being viewed as one mass. This is far less crucial as the total number of plants that are in a group gets bigger; the eye can no longer properly distinguish the variety of plants placed in the grouping.

- **Hedges**

Hedges are a unique way of using trees and shrubs, and it's also the one that involves careful analysis and positioning. Determine the use of hedges if needed for the use in the front yard. Hedges are used to creating a barrier, provide a sense of enclosure, or cover an unacceptable view. Contemplate what degree of maintenance will be necessary for different kinds of hedging plants. Clipped hedges tend to develop a formal view and need routine maintenance. Hedges that are unclipped tend to be more casual or informal; however, they can appear disorganized easily.

Any clustering of plants that are hedges or informal masses is supposed to end at 15 to 20 feet to the edge of the sidewalk/street/road for safety. Plants that are placed closer to the street than this gap will block the car view of the driver.

- **Turf**

The lawn might not be an integral aspect of the front yard. However, it does help to link all elements of the landscape. A well-kept lawn could add to the property's overall attraction. In case a lawn is sought, its outline should be designed together with the majority of the landscape. The lawn must have a well-detailed and uncomplicated shape. Edges of the lawn should be simpler for ease of mowing; curves can be the most convenient to mow around. The lawn is supposed to be as obstacle-free as possible, from bushes, rocks, and birdbaths. Place these inside beds or boundaries. However, lawn might not be a reasonable option for shady areas beneath trees or slopes that are steep. Ground covers for these areas are nicer and easier to sustain.

- **Ground covers**

Placement of plants which mature to a total length of 1 foot may be used for harmony in the lawn or may be used as a replacement instead. A ground cover bed that is planted right next to a lawn or a pavement area may signify an edge of the yard. Continuous ground cover flux will try to unite separate planting regions and aid the eye to travel across the landscape rather comfortably.

- **Flowers**

Flowers that are perennials, annuals, and bulbs are usually favored the most and also the least qualified in creating curb appeal. Like any other species of plants and flowers, they demand strategic positioning in the landscape. However, if the house is profoundly an old-school farmhouse and its residents are devoted gardeners, the secluded farmhouse

garden crowded with the cheerfulness of flowering plants may not be a great idea. Often perennials don't tend to have long bloom duration and are therefore relatively unexciting for the most of growing season.

They are also not present during winters. Annuals bloom for an extended period of time during summer months but are absent during cold weather. Spring flowers offer pleasant spots of color after yet another long winter. However, they are by natural order ephemeral. It is preferable to install them in the less common location of the landscape.

If used with restriction, flowers are beneficial when grown at the bottom of shrubs enclosed by boundaries (do not place flowers among shrubs), or in any containers closer to the entryway. The primary aim of flowers that are in the front yard is to throw a touch of color and appreciation. Pick a simple color scheme for the flowers. Two or a maximum of three organizing or contrasting colors are far more impactful than a rebellion of color.

Flowers should never be the primary component of the landscape. Do not swarm flowerbeds that are in the lawn, and never use flowers for lining driveway. Beds that are in the lawn divert focus from the desired focal point — Flowers filling the driving demand a lot of visual attention to the door of the garage. Perceive flowers as an additional touch, an artifice instead of labeling it as a crucial component in the design. Their finest use may be as room fillers when freshly planted shrubs grow to their mature size.

- **Hard landscaping materials:**

The two main elements of hardscape are the driveway and entrance walk, both typically paved surfaces. If dealing with an existing house or yard, ensure that both of these elements are precisely located on the base plan. After this, decide whether the driveway and walkway are successfully fulfilling their purpose or not. Consider the following general directives for landscaping a newly bought house.

- **Driveway**

The driveway's primary purpose is to give car parking space. For a single-car drive, the minimum usable distance is 10 ft. assess the need for parking zone expansion. If the driveway is also working as the walk from the road and to the front door, then the drive is required to be broadened by 3 ft. or more. Without the additional distance, if a car is pulled up at the drive, there is no space for walking. This pressures the people to walk alongside the slim edge of the car or to stride onto the nearby lawn or plant area. Easy expansion of the drive area will make it easy for people to walk comfortably.

- **Entryway**

There are three important components to the construction of the driveway:

- Giving a secure approach

- Leading people through the landscape

- Impacting their view

Most entrance walks are badly constructed and therefore don't work effectively

Among the most repeated issues is an entry walk that is a little too restricted. Walks are usually 3 feet wide, which compels people to walk one at a time. The walk should be no less than 4 feet wider, in order to manage two people walking side by side. For wheelchair access, it should at least be 5 ft. wider.

The overgrown walk is one related issue. Shrubs grown too near the walk can decrease the width available, and will eventually end up enveloping the walk. Another concern is if the entry walk is unable to be seen clearly. This is especially correct when the walk attaches with the driveway, but there's nothing to demand attention to walk's location. Thoughtful plant placement may and should prompt the eye towards the entry direction.

There is sometimes a lack of aesthetic value alongside the entry walk. An extended lawn expanse and an outline of foundation plantings don't offer a particularly refreshing view. The path to the front door can also be designed to take advantage of differing views. It's not necessary for the walk to be straight in terms of line. Although the walk is meant to be a straight one, one or two turns add excitement and encourage you to change the view of the front doorway. Note, however, if you want the path to curve, it should have some physical cause. Avoid directionless curves, as they can look unnatural and visually unappealing.

- **Area for greeting**

Usually, entry walk comes to an end in front of the front door and often reaches a small-scaled concrete slab that acts as an entrance or area for greeting outside. Space is usually too tight to be working properly. It's so narrow that it makes it uncomfortable for people to step on it while the screen or storm door is opening without getting struck by it or taking a step away. Think about expanding that paving area to comfortably assist two or three persons, at least.

Providing some form of extra protection from elements is also beneficial. The overhead protection prevents you from getting soaked in the rain. You can also contemplate creating a sensation of semi-privacy at the entry. Planting alongside the sides may give a feeling of enclosure. Be mindful of plant sizes and their positioning. However, don't make the error of covering the front door as it won't be seeable from the road.

- **Materials for paving**

The two main factors to consider when selecting paving materials for the entryway, driveway, or area of greeting are the appearance and cost. Concrete is one of the materials that is mostly used for these purposes. Though relatively cheap, it is seldom the most appealing option. There are many varieties of paving materials available, and they can be used to add divergence to the overall landscape and to amplify the property's curb appeal.

Use your house's architectural features and materials for building to assist you in picking appropriate paving materials. If your house is constructed from stone, brick, or wood, then try incorporating the same type of materials into the hardscaping of the landscape. That also amplifies the effect of landscape unity.

Brick is an attractive option for paving and can be used on any paved surface. Brick color and texture give the landscape a visual comfort and are ideal for both formal and informal styles. Bricks add visual interest to the surface of the ground too. They can be laid in any of several patterns or used with other pavements.

Pavers are available readily, and few are quite appealing. Stone is also a great option for pedestrian traffic, and it is especially well suited for an informal look. There are many different stone kinds and categories that are offered. Select a stone that is compatible with regional stone in appearance for the most natural look. Stone is normally not a good choice to be used in driveways unless it is cut thickly and placed on a firm base.

Wood tends to have a desirable texture and natural color. It is ideally suited for informal and modern-looking walks and entry areas. Wood is also a unique material that can be painted and stained to infuse in with other materials. It doesn't suit drives like a stone.

Other paving alternatives could include asphalt, concrete, and gravel. Gravel is an appealing material and tends to give an exciting underfoot texture, but it has to be restraint with edging materials. Concrete is a great option for curvilinear or uneven areas because it can change to any shape. Asphalt should be avoided if possible, as it is utilitarian.

- **Landscape accents**

Accent components that include mostly specimen plants serve as focal points to catch the viewer's attention. They should, therefore, be regarded as adornments and should be used with limitations. An adornment that includes sundials, birdbaths, gazing balls, and obelisks tends to divert attention and diminishes the front yard's unity as well as balance. If you fancy decorative elements, place them in the private backyard area.

Specimen plants can either be trees or shrubs, which serve as focal points due to their exceptional ornamental features. These plants attract attention to themselves by their very nature. The trouble with placing a specimen plant in your front yard is that it becomes the main focal point easily, diverting attention from the door at the front. Therefore, specimen plants should be placed close to the door to avoid this. This will naturally lead the viewer's attention from the plant to the door.

In the front garden, consider using only one specimen tree. More than one will try to compete with one another and with the house. Try to pick a non-overly dominant plant. A shrub with spring flowers or a small tree would be a great choice.

Chapter 4: Healthy gardens and Garden Types

Your garden can be of great help in encouraging and sustaining a comfortable life and can also contribute to your wellness as well as others that may live in the surrounding.

Following are some ideas for maintaining a healthy garden:

- To maintain a healthy garden, the usage of organic materials is of the utmost importance. Organic materials also assist in buffering variations in temperature. For example, organic mulches. There are all different kinds and types of mulches. Some of the common examples are pine bark, wood chips, sawdust, etc. Organic mulches or any kind of vegetation that covers the ground will prevent the soil/ground from rapidly heating up in the hot weather. In cold weather, it would prevent the ground from turning too cold. It also helps maintain the moisture in the soil, minimizes water loss, and provides the plants with necessary nutrients, which is a key in keeping your plants and overall your garden/landscape healthy.

- The trees help to protect against excessive heat and piercing sunlight and also aids in protecting against unfavorable weather conditions, for example, extremely cold winds or frost. Seasonal trees or also known as deciduous trees shed their leaves during winters, inviting the sunlight to keep the surrounding warm and comfortable and regrow their leaves during summer to provide with shade and make the overall temperature cooler, again aiding in the comfort. Be mindful of which kinds of trees you choose and of which variety for your landscape, refrain from choosing roots which are not very invasive. Place your trees with a little bit of distance in accordance with your house-building or paving, so there are fewer chances of root damage. Also, choose your spot carefully, where fallen branches and leaves do not pose a problem and discomfort for you.

- If hard paving is used, then it could get very hot in summers and very cold in winter. Trees keep the paving cold in summer by shading them, especially if the afternoon is too hot. The trick is all about placing the trees in the right places for the utmost comfort. It is a good idea to refrain from placing trees in such areas that they will provide quite a heavy shade in winters, making the sunlight unable to penetrate and the area is further cooled, also the paving beneath might be damp inviting moss and making it slippery too which is quite a problem, especially in extremely cold areas.

- Other structural components can also be used to enhance the comfort and beauty of the landscapes. The use of pergolas outside the building keeps the area sheltered from sunlight and provides an adequate amount of shade, and verandas keep the area cool too. They create favorable conditions for you to relax in your garden and enjoy any kind of weather. There are also cladding materials used and are quite popular too in our modern world. For example, polycarbonate sheeting prevents UV lights and reduces the risk of cancer, even if you're not wearing any sunblock.

- Ventilation also partakes in conserving the quality of air. The fresh air that flows into the house not only takes part in increasing the level of oxygen it also expels excessive carbon dioxide, which has build-up due to the respiration of humans. Moreover, the air that flows through a clean and neat garden into the house will refresh the atmosphere inside the house. If flowers are placed in the garden that smells sweet, the air will be accompanied by pleasant fragrances that will nourish your mood and overall house atmosphere.

- Coming back towards colors. Colors are said to have a psychological impact on you. Colors are set into two groups: warm colors that include orange, red, yellow, and cool colors that include mostly green, blue, pastel colors. Warm colors usually encourage a person psychologically to become active; do work whereas cool colors give an overall relaxing atmosphere. It is a good idea to place warm-colored flowers/plants where you usually work, and cool colored flowers/plants should be placed where you usually sit and relax.

- Scents emitted from many certain plants also have significant medical advantages, for example, herbs such as mints, thyme as they help in clearing nasal activities and prevent any blockage (minutely). They act as decongestants. Whereas some plants may promote allergies such as Amaranth, ordinary sunflowers, daises. Allergies can give hay fever and severe headaches, especially if the ventilation in the garden is not well kept.

- The usage of garden machinery not only causes disturbance to neighbors, who are trying to relax or sleep. It also invests in air pollution, which is definitely not good for health. Instead of making use of machinery, hand tools are a better alternative, and you could always use some extra exercise for refreshment and fitness. For example, usage of axe and handsaw instead of a chainsaw. Usage of hand-pushed mower than a powered land one. Regular cutting keeps the grass healthy and prevents you from the discomfort of cutting long grasses, which is tiring. Avoid using powered trimmers, and use hedging shears in place of it to trim plants. Use a scythe in place of brush cutter.

- Keep any garden machinery you're using well maintained as it will reduce fumes as well as noise and so it does not pose as a disturbance to others.

- The usage of incinerators should be avoided no matter what. It will not only contribute to air pollution, but when the air blows, it will disturb you as well as your neighbors because of the many toxins and fumes it contains that are very harmful to health and is not pleasant in the slightest.

4.1 Formal Garden Design

Formal gardens are architectural, symmetric, impressive, and magnificent. This classic gardening design emerged in Persia, and Islamic classical courtyard gardens, Asian Mughal gardens, renaissance art gardens, elaborate French parterre, and Elizabethan era English knot orchards are all variants of this type. With a few preparation tips and a clear understanding of this style, you will build your own structured backyard privacy.

Advantages of a Formal Garden

At first, formal gardens can appear to entail a lot of effort, but they also deliver some really good landscape advantages.

- This style of garden is suitable for a limited plot because it provides an illusion of scope, bringing beauty to the home.

- Since plantings are small in size, they can be effectively preserved in optimal historical circumstances.

- Except for annual flower beds, all trees and shrubs are central components, keeping recurring costs low.

- The formal garden is really calming for the body and mind.

Planning a Formal-Style Garden

Throughout the design and implementation processes, correct preparation is needed. Consider the scale and form of the greenhouse, its functional intent, and the land's natural features.

Preparing the Land

This will be appropriate to plan the plot for a formal garden. A perfect natural flat landscape. Through earth-moving machinery, slight unevenness may be quickly eroded. When there are significant level variations, plan a two-story stepped garden.

Defining the Perimeter

In a beautifully symmetrical landscape

A square or rectangular plot may be used as it is, but a frequently formed field must be trimmed. Tall hedges or tall walls can divide up the garden area from the plot. The main gate can have to be moved to fall straight from the house's main entrance. That's the garden's central component.

Planning the Layout

Ideally, the model will be drawn on paper with precise proportions because it will be brought to the site for initial execution. For main geometric patterns, select a square, circle, or rectangle. Stretching strings over stakes in the field will help you draw straight lines from the land map. Symmetry is an essential element of any formal garden. Therefore, the areas on either end of the central axis should be designed as mirror images.

When the garden is designed to attract visitors, plan to have wide-open spaces and seating areas you expect. Wrought iron furniture combines with a formal landscape.

Major Features to Include

The following elements distinguish this landscape theme.

Pathways: The central path passes around the main axis, which determines the garden's bilateral symmetry. Other smaller paths can branch off. They may be graved or paved, usually filled with low hedges.

- **Focal point:**

Installed either in the center of the garden or at an end, a water body, an unusual figure, a new sculpture, or a big tree may act as a focal point.

- **Water feature:**

Although water is not so necessary, it is definitely welcome. Consider installing a swimming pond, a stream flowing down the main road, or even a big birdbath.

- **Vertical appeal:**

Establish vertical value by incorporating topiaries, standard-trained or straight-line trees, and stone or stone pillars with decorative or wide urns. Be very sure to use such features to prevent cluttering.

Greenery-Greenery is the foundation of a formal landscape, usually as trimmed hedges, shrubbery, and lawns. This well-manicured appearance is vital. Leave the grass mowed and neatly clipped. Quick-to-shape bushes and plants with naturally smooth forms are favored. Use low-maintenance xerophytes (plants which can tolerate droughts) is a recent phenomenon of informal gardens.

- **Color-** Formal gardens use a minimal paint range. Annual and annual beds may be positioned in rectangular patterns in the center of lawns, or they may be installed around the hedges as one-foot-wide beds. They must be planted together for a pleasant feel using only two to three harmonious colors. You might want to add a few trees as seasonal color highlights.

Plant Suggestions

The following are the plants that work perfectly in a formal garden.

- **Topiary and Hedges**: Yew, rosemary, boxwood, arborvitae, and privet

- **Bushes:** Thuja, ficus, junipers, Brunfelsia, and pencil cypress

- **Trees:** Crabapple, dogwood, cherry and fan palms

- **Annuals:** tulips, salvias, Marigolds, calendulas, asters, and begonias.

- **Low-maintenance plants:** Yucca, cycads, agave and date palms

- **Perennials**: Hydrangea, lavender, nepeta, echinacea, and daffodils.

4.2 Informal Garden Design

Informal gardens are the most growing garden type. With their natural alignment, the intimate garden is also less restrictive. Informal gardening will liberate you from constraints such as awareness of comprehensive horticulture or architecture. And enabling you to 'visit' the gardening before you start, and that's what you must do, and I heartily support gardeners get going with every sort of gardening.

You will see what designs and patterns you want, create planting schemes, notice what works for you and what doesn't. An informal garden must be comfortable and open. Others say casual garden architecture gives more border flexibility and encourages planting to have the foundation instead of hard landscaping.

Though, an informal landscape design should not be confused with gardens that are disjoined, borders that slapdash together, or also features that occur randomly in gardens. Those are things to prevent landscape planners. Even iterating casual doesn't say lazy. During their preparation, open garden architecture requires as much effort and patience as a formal garden—planning, harmony, equilibrium, size, proportion, and correct features and plants in the right position.

Everything seems effortless, though done cautiously.

Looking at UK's adjacent landscapes, you can quickly identify informal landscape projects. Informal implies that the garden implements even looser patterns and curves and typically takes its architecture from land layers. You should trace the site boundary lines, road, house walls, lake, and trees collection and where the sun spreads its warm rays. You can see mixed borders of beautiful plant drifts; perhaps grasses left to plant a seed and dry them out during winter. Far from that of a formal garden's order and its razor accuracy.

Informal gardens are not inclined to follow formal gardens rules, allowing a whole different and unexpected style to blow up. The sky might be the only limit.

How to create an informal garden?

- Mixing different palettes and colors

- Use other products than rough rectangular landscaping

- Adopt curves and smoother lines

- Allow further planting and diversity

- Comfortable and free

- Asymmetrical

- Mixing cohesive materials

Who, do informal gardens are supposed to appeal to?

Informal gardens will cater to fewer regulated citizens who are more in line and appreciate nature on finding its path. Styles for informal gardens like cottage garden and meadow planting encourage plants to mix and develop together.

Although forms should be used, they are not inherently symmetrical or centered on any axis; for example, formal gardens may often be divided in half and might also be combined. In simple words, casual gardens are very comfortable and less deliberate. But this doesn't make them any easier to manage or maintain! Here are some typical conclusions that are recommended for an informal style garden.

Sweeping plants in drifts, blending.

- Keeping it according to the natural topography and lines of the garden

- Natural products for planting and surrounding

- Allowing the garden to grow over a while

- Those who want 'laid back type,' if it's not finished today, it's still tomorrow!

Water features for informal gardens

In gardens that are informal, particularly wildlife or natural ponds, water features are accessible. Use natural materials and gentle curves; natural water will become the garden's emphasis. It is attracting animals and tourists. A poorly built or improperly shaped informal pond will look terrible, making your garden look messy.

Informal landscape management

Maintenance, like every landscape, relies on plants and nature. When you're searching for a home garden filled with summer flowers, make sure that care should be intense, and seed flowers are primed for the season. Though, informal gardens that have slow-growing shrubs and evergreens areas may be comparatively free of maintenance. I typically design casual gardens as a year-round color combination with limited pruning.

The problem of a poorly designed informal garden is that of the 'pick and choose' planting commonly done as people slowly add plants and flowers in their backyard, which bloom at various times, which might end up in a continuous maintenance process. It's also important to carefully consider the height and increasing pace. Anything can start as a lovely little perennial will take over the tiny boundary! A carefully planned garden plan prevents this and provides the landscape a year-round framework that fits your degree of involvement!

The Pitfall of Informal Gardens

Perhaps that is often the undoing of a garden, without order, purpose and preparation an informal garden may only become a catch-all word for "free for all" or "messy garden."

The field above is a perfect illustration of an informal garden, which is a little puzzled. You've got a combination of seasonal shrubs, hedging, and then some fantastic but bonkers trimmed box animals in the middle. Don't misinterpret me as it's quite fun, but it isn't undoubtedly cohesive.

Chapter 5: Themes for landscapes

Just as much as we think of a theme for our homes inside, we often forget to continue it outdoors. A theme can unify your landscape and help lead you in making selections of plants and material. Themes may be as basic as using uniform forms or shapes around your yard, or as complex as designing a soothing garden. The following are a few themes you can consider choosing for your landscape.

5.1 English cottage-style garden

Enjoy the beauty of gardening by giving your yard the English garden design. You may wish to capture the aesthetics of English cottage gardens and celebrate its glory to the fullest or give your home a sense of luxury with English country gardens. By using the simplest technique, you can create a wonderful English garden with no such difficulties.

Generally, English garden designs include one of the two styles: English cottage style or English country style.

Characteristics

These gardens have a well-defined style — a densely planted, informal design, with pathways and hard surfaces built from conventional materials used for building. The effect overall is romantic, artless, and noncontributing.

These days, English cottages are sold for a high price and are the focus of the wealthy society members. A trip through every England village can show an abundance of many cottage gardens; however, they're not limited to only rural areas. There are several common plants in this style in the garden. Naturally, Roses predominate. Hollyhocks that are planted during bygone days next to the cottage walls to keep out moisture appear at the rear of boundaries, cranesbill geranium gives ground cover beneath the trees canopy and variety of perennials, flowers, and annuals that self-seed invests in a burst of colors in all but the months that are coldest.

Choices of plants for the cottage garden

Roses

Some kinds of roses have stems which support themselves, while others might need support. Nevertheless, keep in mind that roses demand an immense amount of care. They have to be pruned, fed, and sprayed for insects and also fungal infections. They are said to be thirsty plants, so you would have to consolidate well-kept manure into soil across the bottom of bushes in autumn. For keeping infestations at minimum, you need to spray plants with specific to rose, specialized fungus, and insect repellent when the April is ending and also spray often until the April has ended.

The Hollyhocks

Hollyhock would be the flower after roses that associate the most with cottage gardens. Plant some hollyhocks and see the last several years, seeding themselves if you forgot to remove the blooms and let all of them grow to 2.4 meters of height.

The drawback of these flowers is only that they're vulnerable to the powdery mildew. But regular fungicide spraying can keep this in check.

The pinks

These gentle and fragrant pinks are easily grown, and their foliage of silvery color gives attraction to the garden throughout the year. They are good for cutting, and they also make a beautiful corsage for special occasions. After about three years, the plants become woody, but it is convenient to keep a continuous flow of plants that are young either by layering shoots that are non-or by taking cuttings.

Lavender

Nothing might be more captivating than the Lavender scent for an English garden. There are many kinds of lavender to pick from that even the gardeners are overwhelmed.

These plants are resistant to any poor soil conditions and drought conditions, making them a worthwhile selection.

Also, they are appealing to bees that make lavender honey from the collected nectar. Grow individual plants to create a hedge or plant them. Flower heads which are dry may be used for baking or for a bowl of potpourri filled with fragrance.

Delphinium

Delphinium is a modern, traditional garden flower. Although the long spikes of the flower are said to be very short-lived, yet they may yield a second flush later in the season if the plants are supposed to be cut back to the land promptly after flowering. Plant the flowers insects of white and blue for the maximum effect. Replenish and grow the stock by splitting the plants after the coming three years or more. Guard against any snails or slugs attacking, especially among new, untried plants.

Clematis

Select many varieties of plants thoughtfully for a range of clematis fumbling over your trellis, fences, or among the trees for several months. Clematis roots have to be shaded from the position of the sun. Place some rocks or just some gravel across the plant's foundation. Three separate classes of pruning are involved; light, severe, and no pruning, so be sure you already know whom yours belongs to so you are able to cut back at the right time of the following year. Look for wilt clematis, or any stem rot, and take any infected stems off.

Nigella

Nigella is commonly known as love-in-the-mist.   It has elegant flowers and leafy ferns like foliage. Each year it plants itself and flowers gorgeously in flower beds. Spread seed wherever a gap lies in the border of the flowers. It blooms for approximately eight weeks.

Verbascum

Verbascum, commonly known as Mullein, requires well-drained soil, plenty of room for the leaves, and sunlight. The various tiny blooms of flowers are produced on spikes that rise in the sandy soil to an altitude of about seven feet.

For a border, plant a stunning perennial, which will also be attractive to bees.

Mock Orange

Mock Orange is a perennial kind of shrub, which is also referred to as Philadelphus because the fragrance from the elegantly rounded stems will encompass the garden throughout the summer evening in June and interact gloriously with the pair Garden Pinks Night and Scented Stocks. Mock Orange grows quite quickly. Mock Orange must be properly pruned. The stems of dead flower must be cut out right after flowering, and also cut any old branches to avoid overcrowding.

Elements for English cottage garden

Walkways

As an essential part of the garden design, the cottage garden's curvy walkways make the seating areas and flower beds convenient to reach. They could be some slim mud or a gravel road bordered by bricks or might be a number of plantations that function as a boundary.

Lawns

Lawns are not a necessary part of the cottage gardens. However, unplanted areas can be covered with grass to match your personal requirements. In order to preserve the informal character, curvy lines can be superior to lines that are straight.

Garden structures

- The cottage garden structures are made from either iron or wood. They are lined with trellises, climbers, arches, and also fences.

- Roses are the typical favorite option of climbing, but other floral climbers such as climbing or clematis can also be equally beautiful. To plant near seating areas, choose climbers with fragrant flowers, for example, jasmine and sweet pea.

- In areas with a great view of the garden, iron or wooden benches can be installed. Visual significance can also be created by statues and sculptures.

- The transformation of any garden to the English cottage-style garden has nothing like a picket fence. I painted in blue and white color, the seating area, and flower beds within a lawn can be a perfect backdrop.

Flowers, beds, shrubs, and trees

Perennials plants are said to be the foundation of the flower beds, including a handful of annuals that are added for attraction. These are grown together in order to give a group of colors when they bloom. Glassy, attractive flowers are fancied, but the cottage gardeners shut out ponderous color schemes. A few plants with heavy foliage for texture and color, some kitchen herbs, a chest of medicine, and a variety of fruits and vegetables finishes the picture. The front consists of shorter plants, and larger plants are moved to the backside of the flower bed. Some fruit trees can be splayed against a wall in the minimum space to bring maximum fruit.

5.2 English country style garden

For English cottage gardens where chaos predominates more freely, English country gardens are all about order. Cleanly cut hedges, evidently defined bed edges, and healthy swaths of lavish green gardens foster the aura of an English country garden and are readily adapted to any size yard. There are a variety of garden areas linked by paths in an English country garden. Every area of the garden presents neatly kept gardens or natural-looking landscapes.

One area might have a beautiful pool, surrounded by leafy trees, which reflects brilliant autumn leaf tones in the water. Another could show well-cut hedges or even topiaries. A luxuriant hedgerow, or a forest swath, surrounded by a stone grotto and waterfall, might all be part of an English country garden. These gardens were designed for luxuriant country estates and are built to be experienced on foot. Include a focal point, such as a trellis, water, the topiary or statue, in each area. You may not have a sophisticated folly or a garden structure, but you can add a pergola or a gazebo to your garden. Focal points need not be large to be effective; they only need to be placed in such a way that they demand and draw attention.

Include the whole yard with seating areas. Strategically place them to maximize carefully planned perspectives. English country garden, like decorative stone benches, usually have formal seats. Choose benches made of iron or weather-resistant wood in a modern setting, featuring classic designs that add the English style to your garden.

Choices of plants for a country garden

Japanese Anemone

Japanese anemone is a tall, stately, perennial anemone that produces brilliant foliage and large, subdued flora in shades from pure white to creamy pink, each with its own green button in the center. Seek blooms during the summer and fall, often until the first freezing period. They are a cinch to grow and are adaptable to the most growing conditions.

Ageratum

Ageratum is grown for its whimsical flowers, mostly in shades of blue though other colors may include pink, lavender, white and red. These famous bedding plants are most commonly bought as nursery begins in packs or in flats but can also be grown from seed. Ageratum can be grown in tubes, used as an edging along paths or boundaries, or massed in displays, ranging from a couple of inches high up to three feet tall.

Dusty Miller

An interesting landscape addition, grown for its silvery grey foliage, is the dusty miller plant. The beautiful leaves of the dusty miller plant are appealing companions for the other blooms in the gardens. The care for dusty miller is minimal when established.

Gaura

Gaura lindheimeri can range from 15 to 4 meters high, also known as a wallflower, whirling butterfly, and bee flowers, but most new cultivars are grown to make them compact and container- safe. The long bloom time is much longer than most perennials, one of the best features of Gaura plants. The heaviest blooms occur early in summer, but flushes of flowers can be expected to recur during the summer. Gaura leaves are lance-shaped and, depending on the form, often tinged with purple, cream, or gold.

Daylily

Daylilies are widely known, easy to grow, low-maintenance perennials that are tough, long-lasting, and can be neglected. It blooms profusely, although each flower lasts only one day, and there are tens of thousands of varieties. In comparison to the true lily that comes from bulbs, daylilies emerge from fleshly roots. Plants may start flowering in mid-spring, and some may continue until fall, depending on the type.

Iris

Stir up the color of the spring with iris flowers. This broad range of bloomers includes plants that grow from a bulb. There are also re-blooming irises in which multiple floral displays are produced during the growing year. The petals look like a classic sign of fleur de lis. Some petals are rising up while others cascade down. The petals at the center stand upright and botanically are known as standards. These tall petals are like flags of signal, waving in potential pollinators.

Lupine

The flower garden may be shaded by purple, pink, red, white and yellow by the thick floral spikes of the lupines. The foliage is similar to palm leaves, each with seven to ten leaflet segments. Lupine blossoms are rich nectar stores that become favorite among bees and butterflies. Plant them alongside other favorites of early summer butterflies, such as poppies, penstemon, and alliums, which prosper in similar conditions. Lupines are an appealing addition to wildflower gardens and meadows, but they also adapt easily to the perennial border.

Snapdragon

The bright colored spiky flower stalks make a nice foil that's like Brunner and bleeding heart, for the cooler shades of most spring flowers. Planting them into clusters can contribute to the border transition from spring to peak hot season. The pale yellow variations are the easiest to mix with roses, purples, and even reds in a combination. Breeders have been experimenting with snapdragons for many years now, and there are trailing and creeping varieties that have now become widely available. There are good filler plants for baskets and containers.

Tulips

Perhaps the most emblematic of flowers are tulips. The classic cup shape is recognized by all. It is freely used by artists and graphic designers — abstract, literal, and romanticized in drawings, paintings, paper patterns, and advertising too. You may find them in many unexpected locations while looking for them. Blossoming ranges from a 4-6-week window, which relies entirely on spring temperatures.

You can create a pageant that runs long or a single color explosion through careful selection. The colors red, pink, yellow, purple, orange, white forms the basic palette. But more colors like mauve, ivory, citron, cherry, and blush are also available.

Elements for English country garden

Pathways

Well-used pathways in the grass can lead to various elements that are of interest to the garden. It's not paved.

Hedges

Clipped, shaped hedges, and also topiaries are deliberately presented in such a way that the landscape is open, spacious, and natural.

Lawns

The vast majority of these garden styles are lawn areas modeled after the undulating grasslands of the countryside.

Garden Features

It is common to have a garden layout like a Greek monopteros or Chinese pavilion. The statues, sculptures, or carefully built ruins provide a great value of interest to the overall landscape.

Flowers, beds, shrubs, and trees

In the usual landscape design of the English country garden flower beds and pruned shrubs have no room. A combination of native shrubs is left to grow and spread naturally along the edge of the water. It may be necessary to trim occasionally.

Indigenous trees are superior to imported plants from distant lands and what is naturally growing in the surrounding areas. They are located in close proximity to a natural grove.

5.3 Japanese Zen style

Zen gardens, popular as the Japanese rock garden, draw people who prefer sand carefully controlled settings of raked or rocks and shrubs specifically chopped. You should think about a more conventional or natural Gardens if you consider harmony and serenity more often in the environment of the forest and feel harmony when surrounded by wildflowers and soft-texture plants. Zen gardens emphasize natural values (Shizen), plain (Kanso), and discipline (Koko). Zen Buddhist monks established the first Zen Gardens in the sixth century to aid in meditation. Later they began teaching Zen principles and concepts using the gardens. Over the years, the garden has been designed and structured, but its fundamental structure remains unchanged.

How to create a Japanese Zen style garden?

The main areas of a Zen garden are carefully raked sand or gravel with precise rocks. The sea is depicted by sand raked in an oval, spiral, or rippled shape. To create a soothing pattern, place the rocks above the sand. You can add plants but minimize them and use plants that stretch and are low rather than upright. Introspection and meditation should be encouraged.

One of the most important architectural elements is the symbolism of the stones in the Zen garden. Top of upright rocks can represent trees, while smooth, horizontal stones represent water. Fire is depicted by arching stones. Test various layouts to see what the design refers to. The garden can also have a simple bridge or path with rock or stone lanterns. Both features provide a sense of space and can be used as a medium for meditation. The term 'shakkei' refers to the landscape borrowed and refers to the practice of using the landscape around it to make the garden appear beyond its borders. A Zen garden shouldn't have a pond or body of water next to it.

Choices of plants for Japanese Zen garden

Azalea (Rhododendron)

Japanese gardeners have been cultivating azaleas for hundreds of years, rewarding them with their pink, yellow, salmon, red, purple, and white trumpet-shaped spring flowers. Modern hybridists have developed an azalea that is blooming, so you don't have to expect the floral feast of this perennial shrub for another spring. Give your azalea shrub a partly shaded site; change the floor to increase acidity with organic materials such as compost or leaf mold. Azaleas like regular humidity, but in wet winter soil, they can rot.

Camellia

Planting a Japanese Camellia in the garden may be the start of a life-long love tale, as these sluggish growers will live in the garden for centuries. The landscape lightens up with big, beautiful petaled blooms with glossy foliage of Camellia in certain winter months, given you live in zone 6 or warmer place.

Cherry blossom tree

Place an ornamental cherry tree, and for many seasons to come, you will enjoy four seasons of elegance. White or pink spring flowers typically have a smell of almonds and attract hungry bees from hibernation. Shortly after, bright green leaves provide an enticing border anchor, and particularly on weeping specimens. Fall and winter will signify the beautiful bark if you have grown the paperbark cherry with a striated appearance with a bark of reddish colors.

Wisteria (Wisteria Sinensis)

You should not be a victim of your own performance when taking care of a wisteria tree. The tipping point, where it seems like the plant could take over the earth, maybe a mature wisteria. Put the floribunda of the giant next to its support structure after flowering. This regulates the production and makes it easier to see blooms. You may not even need any support because you can train the Japanese wisteria as a tree, which limits growth with biannual pruning to several limbs.

Hydrangea

They are famous ornamental plants found in Japan, particularly the macrophylla kind, which color switches between blue and pink depending on the acidity of the soil. Hydrangeas are in their most luscious form in climates with gentle summers and sufficient rainfall. If your region has dry seasons and summers that are quite hot, choose the paniculata varieties which are most accepting of bad weather than the kinds which have big leaves.

Things/elements needed for Japanese Zen garden

Sand or gravel

The flat surface of a Zen garden contains crowned granite, fine gravel, or small steeples. These particles should not be round but angular so that they can be separated into patterns. Dunker sand or gravel performs best in a poorly lit environment than light materials because it can reflect less sunlight.

Stone forms

In Zen garden wherein big rocks are strategically positioned on a flat surface, the stone has a significant role. A number of stone types include different elements, including water, metal, air, fire, and earth. High upright stones represent trees and wood, while low upright stones represent metal. Stones of a branch or arching form are fire, and wide flat stones are water. Lying stones represent the earth as they appear to be relaxed and tranquil.

Arrangements of rock

A Zen garden, along with sand or stone, frequently uses a rock to create a more abstract view of a wider landscape. The sand is seen as representing water, and the rocks can be used to represent a mountain or an island. Rocks may also symbolize animals in the shape of a tortoise, cranes, or other species. These animals tend to represent longevity. Zen garden rocks are usually light or dark grey with a weathered look. Sand or gravel is often raked or collected carefully to produce a ripple-like effect.

Enclosure

Zen gardens are also enclosed by a fence for privacy and harmony in the garden. The enclosure may be given a form of a stone wall or a group of stones signifying the edges.

Structural elements

Zen gardens can have structural elements such as walkways, bridges, and lanterns. Bridges enable people to have a look at the garden from a different angle. A bridge may only consist of flat stone slabs, representing an arch over which visitors can walk. The Zen garden also has a clearly specified line of lower steps.

Lanterns are found more suitable than metal in the natural setting of the garden, typically made of wood or stone.

5.4 American southwest style

The Southwest garden reflects the dry arid areas of the west. Similarly, you don't need to stay in certain areas to admirer and incorporate their elegance into your own yard. The southwestern style is recognized for its Native American and Spanish specifics that add to the overall plain, practical, and small maintenance landscape. This style contains local vegetation, which uses vivid, decorative construction materials.

Elements within Southwest gardens:

- Terracotta tiles

- Fountains

- Native American decor

- Olla pottery

- Red clay pavers

- Plaster

- Gravel

- Natural stone

- Decomposed Granite

- Desert hues

- Wood

When something relates to hardscaping materials, go for shades like orange, red, brown, and yellow that are also used in the sunset or natural ecosystems of the Southwest. Using common structures materials in places including walkways, driveways, and walls to ensure a smooth flow in the project. Decomposed granite is accessible in several desert color selections and is a perfect material alternative for walkways. Use exclusive, vividly colored decoration, and plantings can make the landscape shine in areas and bring charm to your yard.

Basic elements within a Southwest garden:

1. **Patio** - areas are an essential component within this design theme. A shaded environment is a must, particularly in places of intense heat in summers. Many patios have a

wide shaded seating area that is an expansion of your home living room.

2. **Dry creek bed** - is a perfect way to reflect water inside your southwest landscape theme. River rock may be spread intermixed with various shaped rocks and boulders with natural, drought-resistant plantings around the margins.

3. **Terracing** - is advised in places where topography becomes sloped. Construction materials like rocks, railroad ties, or boulders may be used to add to the southwestern layout.

4. **Lawns** - are typically not built into a southwest garden when the homeowner has kids or dogs in need of any free play area. However, others may like the look of including grass in their design. Plan a limited area with a turf plant that is drought resistant, or you have the choice of utilizing artificial turf too, though.

5. **Colorful plantings** - that are natural and woody are suitable for this southwest plant color scheme. Flowering shrubs that draw birds and other wildlife blend beautifully with the desert painted hardscape stuff.

6. **Lighting** - is critical when showing off the attraction of the southwest layout in the evening as well. Lighting design improves the tone, form, and plant species used in your design.

7. **Fire pits.** In this design, twilight is one of the very alluring moments to appreciate the yard. Fire pits and outdoor fireplaces bring welcoming energy to meeting areas.

8. **Water features.** Desert gardens that are environmentally sustainable accept water as a source of life that must be treasured and enjoyed. Whereas wide artificial fountains and large pools may be appealing components, the loss of water by evaporation and also the additives used to maintain them free of algae render them as less sustainable. Water features that are smaller such as rotating fountains lose less water by evaporation, which can be simpler and much more ecologically conscious key points for such a Southwest landscape.

The Southwest theme brings luxury to your house by expanding your outdoor living room with a large enclosed deck, furnished in hanging and planted plants, wall art, and decorative accessories. When you do plan to include water in your environment, do it carefully; southwest ecosystems need minimum water to create a major effect. Elements such as birdbaths and water fountains are the best choice to integrate water as a feature in your design. With minimal natural resources, this landscaping design has grown in popularity within suburban landscapes as it preserves water while providing a distinct rustic appeal.

Plant Types

All types of cactus. The hardest plants in the Southwest, i.e. cactuses, have adapted to survive in extreme conditions. Their spongy, sculptural shapes, built to hold water over long stretches of drought, maybe contrasted against the background of fences or walls. Here, vertical Mexican organ pipe and golden barrel (species of cactus) build confident scenery in an entranceway in Phoenix.

Grasses, Shrubs, and perennials Plants that are native desserts are possibly the best-adapted to the Southwestern environments, and if you desire to have more variety in your landscape, consider the plants from several other arid areas. The aim is to search for those who survive with a minimum amount of water and also in fast-draining soils of desserts. In this landscape of Santa Fe, in New Mexico, the designer developed a vibrant look with plants that are tolerant of droughts such as coneflowers with white petals, ears of silvery lambs, and AstroTurf.

Shade trees. Build warm pools of shaded areas in the garden with Southwestern tree branches. Palo verde, desert willow, chitalpa, and all sorts of the mesquite are fine low-water choices.

Cooling blues: Plants that are used with leaves or flowers in the color of brown, blue, purple, and silver may have a cooling impact in a dry landscape of Southwestern dessert. Shrubby germander is a fine drought-tolerant choice with lavender-colored flowering and gray leaves preferred by hummingbirds. This common sotol provides a cooling effect.

Fall color. The high-elevation landscapes of southwest welcome seasonal transition with plants that are chosen to transform from green to gold and to dark bronze. This landscape in Albuquerque, skunk bush, New Mexico, sumac puts a spectacular autumn display. A rugged Western shrub called skunk bush sumac, it grows to around 5 feet tall by 8-feet long. The gray and somewhat green foliage turns to bright red and gold in autumn.

Garden Accessories

Iconic motifs: Southwest is abundant with ancient icons, from diamond-shaped Native American weaves to longhorn steering heads and lessons. To integrate the region's classic photographs into your design, search for elements that are natural to view on garden gate or walls. The front door includes a typical line of pepper and a bell of rustic-style.

Metal art garden: Steel flower sculptures like prickled pear cactus by the gate brings surprises to the garden year-round. Densely planted desert plants cause statues to stand out.

5.5 Tropical or Semi-Tropical Style

Lush landscapes are lined with big, brightly colored flowers and shrubs. There are also bats, lakes, and butterflies. Water and plants are everywhere. Mats of falling leaves and dirt composting the ground. Strong aromas fill the room.

Each of these habitats should be simple to take care of the ecosystems they have created, and hard to take on in international climates. Since the general atmosphere of a region so strongly influences a landscape's wellbeing, a successful planner should first tackle the overall look, before evaluating and designing the different micro-climates of a site, keeping in mind that landscape types may be mixed and balanced under some circumstances.

Tropical planting

You don't have to fly to the tropical Asian or South Pacific Island to avoid the stresses of daily life — if you already have a garden resort-style, which is like an everyday vacation.

In Australia's subtropical and tropical areas, a rising pattern for gardens resembles the lush scenery of that of a five-star resort we have always been dreaming of.

How To Design A Tropical Garden?

1. Colorful views, focal points, and linear paths develop the garden layout and also helps to link the outdoor and indoor spaces.

2. Formal pathways and plain flower beds usually contrast with forest plantings, whereas luscious trees, vivid plants, wooden furniture, brightly colored, and Balinese lanterns cushions finish the theme of the resort.

3. The entry of the garden is significant as you've heard the first impression is the last impression. Playing with the minds of viewers is also an art, bringing the garden a good amount of pleasure.

The trip through our living conditions will be as fun as the goal of life.

How To Layer Tropical Foliage

To build excitement year-round, tropical gardens focus on vegetation instead of flowers.

Vegetation should be flashy, vibrant, and vivid, and plants should be picked based on leaf scale, form, and texture.

Planting in sets of the odd numbers (3, 5, 7, and 9) is a popular technique used by the garden designers — offers a large brushstroke of texture and color, creating a big change to the garden look.

Placing plants alongside should generate suspense and attraction.

Place plants with yellow, red, pink, purple, orange, and lemon juice-green leaves next to each other for optimal effect.

Brightly colored flowers like fragrant frangipani, divine hibiscus, decorative ginger, and spectacular hemp lilies can light the garden and contrast the vivid soil-dwelling leaves and lush canopy.

Tropical Trees For The Backyards

A collection of beautifully arranged bamboos and plants is a key to your backyard's tropical feel.

While frequently mocked for growing undesirably large or fleeing, palms and bamboo can support the garden's look and mood — they also provide rustle of vegetation in the breeze, fill the garden with the fern-like roof, and thick green colored walls will do a fantastic screening for privacy.

There are a billion varieties to pick from, so contact a professional bamboo or palm nursery to get professional advice.

Be mindful as not all species match every area, so smaller or miniature plants are the better option for small-sized gardens and courtyards.

EDIBLE TROPICAL PLANTS TO TRY

To cook, try planting Asian herbs and Asian spices in the tropical garden.

They not only add beautiful tastes as well as aromas to a large variety of foods but smell great in the greenhouse and also discourage pests.

Kaffir lime, Cardamom, coriander, lemongrass, and mint grow well in cool, moist spots with tropical shrubs.

In March or April, edible ginger planted during spring will be ready to harvest — just grow a healthy-looking store ginger rhizome.

To harvest, dig clumps.

HOW TO PREPARE THE SOIL FOR A TROPICAL GARDEN?

Gardens in subtropical and tropical regions need a particular approach to a temperate climate.

Tropical gardeners don't really dig into plants. However, they are required for the layering soil with fertilizer, leaf mold, garden cuttings, and also mulch.

The layering of leaf mulch is a method found naturally in gullies and forests, where soil productivity remains in the top several inches.

HOW TO MAINTAIN TROPICAL GARDEN?

The perfect time to plant in tropical areas is early in the morning before humidity and heat have built up.

I was taking a stroll through the garden every morning, pruning and ending at the shredder. The shredded pruning content will be composted and added to the field for the natural process. Do not expect a maintenance-free tropical garden.

Anybody who is gardening in a dry, high-rainfall environment knows that during rainy times, plants erupt off the field.

They should be cut back into submitting, or they might take over. Need for frequent housekeeping requires a decent pair of dryers — using them to constantly brush up any dried seeds, dead palm grass, and discarded flowers.

Fill your garden with organic mulches and fertilizers every spring. Spray all of the leaves with a solution of seaweed every season for keeping the plants vigorous and strong.

For tropical gardens, the area of lawn must be small-time people spend weeding and mowing is a waste of time!

Shiny-leafed bromeliads will also impress you with the help of their strength and vigor.

Although they might bloom only once, they continue to develop, sprouting new pups. When a pup exceeds 10 cm, break it with a knife, then again plant it in the pine bark and not the soil.

Instead, it keeps the plant naturally clumping. Bromeliads do not have to grow in the greenhouse or garden, they're just as excited to be with the trunks of trees and pots.

Most gingers that are ornamental die during winter, and the shaggy, rotting leaves will be removed.

Whenever the weather heats, feed them any aging compost as soon as new leaves emerge. Gingers require daily watering in the growing season.

5.6 Mediterranean Landscape Style

If you're always thinking of a Mediterranean holiday, this landscape theme is for you. With both the right plants, fabrics, and accessories, you will add Mediterranean charm to your backyard.

Mediterranean landscapes are well recognized for beauty. Inspired by Italy, Spain, and France, this garden theme blends natural materials and plants with traditional decorations and designs. Terracotta pots, fountains, statuary, and bocce ball courts Roman columns are all Mediterranean gardens. A Mediterranean landscape's plant palette consists of plants that offer texture, color, and structure — think, cypress trees, ornamental grasses, and lavender.

Mediterranean-inspired scenery can take you to another place once you walk out. The fragrance of fragrant flowers, the sound of dripping water, and the soft color of terracotta make you want to settle down and enjoy wine. What you'll lose is a glittering blue ocean shot.

HOW TO CREATE A MEDITERRANEAN-STYLE GARDEN?

Many Mediterranean styled gardens are fragrant from plants that are myrtle lavender, rose, and jasmine. Also, the large cypress Italian trees, seen throughout the Mediterranean garden, possess a distinct sage wood fragrance that brings you on a trip through colder climates. Many silver leaf varieties can also be used in the Mediterranean planting. These mostly include Helichrysum italicum Artemisia' Powis House,' numerous phlomis types, and byzantine fluffy, feathery Stachys.

Frequent planting is quite common in Mediterranean gardens. There's fantastic French lavender or cotton lavender drifts, and after they've flowered, they're formed into tidy mounds. This method of planting brings architectural value after flowering that is used for a great impact. You may divide mounds with a variety of bulbs, like alliums, offering variety and height.

Put up a pergola Mediterranean garden also has a pergola or, in other words, a protected field. It offers relief on hot summer days. It is also an ideal canopy to indulge alfresco in hot weather. The frames are mostly constructed from older branches of trees and wrapped in brushwood or wood canopy.

Building your own wood pergola is simple, and there are also several self-assemble sets in the stores and markets. You may also purchase natural brushwood filtering plates, which may be used in covering existing roofs also to finish the Mediterranean theme.

There's an abundance of plants which can develop beautifully on a pergola, like several vines, and you might try campsis, also called the trumpet vine, for a very exotic look; 'Madame Galen' is a strong plant type and one that's doing really well here.

Gravel

Gravel is a perfect option for Mediterranean styled garden, reflecting light and heat, contributing to the aura.

Gravel gardens perform well in complete light, open area. When planting, you should use a plantation barrier above the soil to prevent the weeds from developing between the plants.

Plants growing in gravel contain herbs. Most of them occur in the Mediterranean garden and enjoy having pebbles around them, and also have them mixed in the soil for excess drainage. Gravel may also be looked at as a low-maintenance garden, and, besides being the ideal choice for herbs, it extends itself to plant species such as euphoria, lavender, cistus, eryngium, hebe, agapanthus, and Stachys.

Plant some pots

Pots are a perfect choice for the Mediterranean. Try and stick to the right look with the terracotta and big Cretan style urns. You can also add some glossed plant pots if you really like them. I have also put big vacant terracotta and olive jars in the garden for decoration or focal point in between and also on the terrace.

Selecting what kind of plants to place in the pots may be a minefield, so I would suggest single types of perennials like Pelargonium or shrubs that are single or trees like a bay.

Keep the gardening simple, because you need to put all of the plants inside during colder months. Plants like oleander bougainvillea and citrus both require winter protection, and so it's a wise choice to be using a single plant while creating larger pots.

Tile with terracotta

Search for a Mediterranean paving type terracotta. The stone's soft tones will quickly carry you into a warmer climate.

With this much variety and option in the market now, from reconstructed tiles that look quite similar to terracotta, you only need to try out a few other samples which work best.

Pick terracotta pavement with a smashed edge for a unique look; for a smoother appearance, pick a tile that can be placed to follow a pattern as shown in this area, making an outdoor styled carpet in the middle which might also be suitable for a chair and table. In paved areas, laying terracotta stones in the diamond styled pattern often helps to establish a more natural look.

Accessorize potting, a wall fountain, rustic furniture, and fragranced plants.

The walls

The walls of the garden, either made of stone or brick, will help you build a small oasis or Mediterranean garden space. When you have hideous walls, paint them to a very smooth, tropical tone to cover up the heat of the Mediterranean. There are too many paint shades you can pick for outdoor use.

The walls will help secure the tenderer plants, so you will also be able to grow many climbers that are scented.

Trachelospermum jasminoides, which is a perfect choice for a climber, is being used in perfume production, and it also grows in southern France. These climbers are now readily accessible in the UK as huge climbing plants and can be taught to expand horizontally along the wall for a great effect.

Consider planting an olive tree.

While thinking of a traditional Mediterranean plant, the olive tree is the first one to take up the seat. Olive trees have been quite famous with the garden designers, and they are also often used on showcase in restaurants.

Olea europaea is a variety of olive trees that you may come across in the garden centers. Place it in the spot which is most exposed to the sunlight, sheltered from the north and the northeast storms, to ensure your tree grows healthy. Plant in soil that will not get waterlogged. Olives may be planted in alkaline or acidic soil, but do not like clay and they need extra drainage.

Olives grow quite efficiently in pots with a decent mix of multi-purpose manure, so don't flood the tree with an unnecessarily big container while re-potting.

When your olive has been potted, ensure the roots do not freeze in winter because this can contribute to poor growth. Also, use seaweed feed between May and September and do it in the late spring, not in winters, if you want to prune lightly.

Add a water feature.

Water features are definitive components to be added in a Mediterranean garden to reduce the summer heat. Water often adds another aspect to a garden — the soft movement of flowing water and its reflecting qualities contribute to the overall atmosphere.

Several small water bodies are accessible for gardens today.

You can also opt to purchase a fountain wall with a stone trough beside it for the water to flow through. You can also purchase wall fountains that are self-contained in terracotta, marble, lead, and steel.

You can always attempt to create a water feature on your own: get a big pot, measure the water volume, so you have the pump of the right size, ensure the pot is also watertight and flat, and place it over the pool that can be dressed with pebbles.

Evaporation may occur where there are water features, particularly those with a wide surface area. When plants stay in the water, look for 'wicking' - where a flower or stem head absorbs water; be sure that you don't overplant alongside the water feature's edge.

Celebrate a slope

If the garden is on a terrace, on a hill, several Mediterranean plants can be cultivated ideally. Placing big rocks from the nearby quarry throughout the whole terrace can retain its beautiful and natural look. You may grow several smaller alpine or small-flowering perennial varieties, which include Helianthemum and Erigeron. The plants would shortly naturalize, cascading over the rocks, and they will self-seed.

Series of stone steps that lead up by planting that are interspersed with shrubs and trees can be planted with a different variety of roses. Other plants, for example, the Stipa gigantea, will contribute to the overall Mediterranean aura.

Rustle up an outdoor retreat

We should all dream of creating a lovely outdoor space surrounded by gorgeous scented plants – and sunny summers! We don't always have high temperatures throughout the summer. However, we can still develop our own small piece of Mediterranean paradise with some important elements, even if we don't have a rustic stone retreat. Garden centers also have several fire pit types available, which will look fantastic in a courtyard environment supported by rustic metal chairs. Try placing storm candles near seating areas and burning citronella

Lanterns that will ward off any undesired flying pests and smell amazing. Place huge outdoor paving cushions for casual seating, and use warm throws on cold summer nights.

Chapter 6: Benefits of Home landscaping

Flowers draw our attention to their appealing view, lively colors... and shrubs entertain us with those soothing scents. The views and aromas of the landscapes and lawns are easy to appreciate, but do you realize that their true meaning is far greater than aesthetics and fragrances? Well maintained landscapes provide huge advantages for people as well as the environment. Let's discuss some of the landscapes' least known but important benefits.

6.1 Environmental Benefits

Grass, rather than cement and asphalt, is much cooler. It functions as an "air conditioner" for the nearby area.

Moreover, lawns tend to be 31 degrees cooler than the asphalt and its 20 degrees cooler as compared to bare soil.

- Trees that shade homes can decrease temperature up to 40 degrees.

- Grass plays an important role in removing and capturing dust, particles of smoke, and any other pollutants there might be. It also produces oxygen.

- Healthy and well-maintained lawns absorb toxic runoff that may potentially be filtered into water bodies.

- Grasses absorb and break down carbon dioxide into oxygen. A 50'x50 'lawn typically supplies a family with four members with an ample amount of oxygen.

- Plants and lawns significantly decrease noise pollution; As compared to hard surfaces like concrete and paving, they can decrease the noise by 20 to 30%. Turfgrass delays and soaks up runoff into water bodies.

It is essential that landscapes and lawns continue to exist as a viable part of well-maintained communities, particularly in those areas where water is restricted and has drought problems. There are quite a few techniques that can help manage landscapes and lawns to limit water demand and still provide significant environmental benefits.

6.2 Physical and Psychological Benefits

There are detailed research and data on the effects of human contact with trees, plants, and grass. Studies have found that by communicating with nature and by simply viewing it, people experience emotional relief and relaxation. Harvard Health Publications says children that suffer from ADHD tend to have a greater concentration after visiting outdoors. Workers work more efficiently, and their cognitive function is also increased when employed in environments that have a lot of greenery.

But the most important factor is what people instinctively experience and feel about plants and greenery in their lives – that if it enhances their life's quality and comfort if they want to make an effort to better their lifestyles.

Conclusion

Landscapes are essential because they significantly contribute to our well-being and living conditions. They provide a wider context to our lifestyles. Our feeling of well-being is enhanced by residing in aesthetically appealing landscapes that also provides us with a sense of spirituality. Most underdeveloped landscapes allow people to communicate with nature, to revive their bodies and minds and they gain a greater appreciation for the nature.

A well-maintained landscape is a wonderful vision. This not only helps you to feel at home, it also offers compliments from family and friends. Landscapes are constructed to enhance a person's way of living and to provide them with utmost relaxation and comfort. It not only gives you a sense of wellbeing, a well-maintained landscape also beautifies your residence's overall appearance.

Create your ideal landscape with proper sets of principles, ideas and inspiration you have gathered. For more practical experience, you can visit other people's houses. Note how they have decorated their landscape, which elements they have chosen and how have they placed them to match the theme and what kind of theme have they designed their landscape in. Think about what extra entertainment you can add, which would not only suit your need but would provide your landscape with another level of excitement.

Designing landscapes is all about one's personal desire and how effectively do they put their art in practical use to create their ideal landscape.

Made in the USA
Coppell, TX
10 April 2021

53459345R00095